BUSINESS DEVELOPMENT SERIES

COMMUNITY CREDIT UNIONS

Produced by CUNA's Center for Professional Development and the National Association of Community Credit Unions (NACCU). The NACCU is a professional network of community credit union staff and directors. As an organization, NACCU members promote and leverage group strength to support the mission of community credit unions. For more information on the National Association of Community Credit Unions, please call (800) 356-9655, ext. 4033, e-mail mmuckian@cuna.com, or visit the NACCU web site at www.cuna.org (click on "community credit unions").

Product #22895

Lucy Harr

CUNA & Affiliates

KENDALL/HUNT PUBLISHING COMPANY
4050 Westmark Drive   Dubuque, Iowa 52002

Written by Lucy Harr
Produced by Patty Lucas and Beth Stetenfeld
Production assistance by Elaine Harrop and Rachel Imsland

Printed in the United States of America
10   9   8   7   6   5   4   3   2   1

CONTENTS

ACKNOWLEDGMENTS

Many thanks to the following individuals who willingly gave their time, efforts, and expertise to the development of this publication: Maria Berkowitz, Central Appalachia People's Federal Credit Union; Nancy Bryant, 1st City Savings Federal Credit Union; John Carpio, Decibel Credit Union; Susan Cusick, Novi Community Credit Union; Colleen Doster, Arrowhead Credit Union; Bill Farley, Central Virginia Federal Credit Union; Joyce Harris, Heartland Credit Union; Betty Mathiessen, credit union consultant; Michael Teator, Kraft Foods Federal Credit Union; Tom Wanttie, Aberdeen Federal Credit Union; and Rich Woldt, CUNA Mutual Group.

A special thanks to the National Association of Community Credit Unions (NACCU) for cosponsoring this handbook. In particular, sincere gratitude to the following NACCU members: NACCU cofounders Gary Base, Community Credit Union, and Charlie Grossklaus, Royal Credit Union; and board members Ray Burnett, Mid-Minnesota Federal Credit Union, and Bob Hoefer, Dupaco Community Credit Union; and Mike Muckian, director of NACCU administration.

Others involved in the production of this handbook: Elaine Harrop, Rachel Imsland, Jim Jerving, Patty Lucas (consultant), Mike McLain, Beth Stetenfeld, and Tricia Tooman of CUNA & Affiliates.

ABOUT THE AUTHOR

Lucy Harr is a former CUNA executive with more than twenty years of experience in the communications field, most of it spent helping credit unions. She is the owner of Providing Solutions, a writing and consulting firm, and a partner in Fourth Lake Communications, LLP, a partnership specializing in guides for credit unions.

INTRODUCTION

Not since the passage of the Federal Credit Union Act in 1934 has there been such enormous potential for Americans to participate in the benefits of a credit union. The Credit Union Membership Access Act (H.R. 1151) has reopened the door slammed shut by banker lawsuits. In 1999, federal community charters added about 11 million potential members, and federal occupational charters added more than 1.5 million potential members through select employee groups (SEGs). Just seven of the anticipated charter requests were expected to reach a combined potential membership of 4.6 million. State regulators are acting on requests for charter conversions as well. These newly minted community charters will join about 1,000 other community credit unions in providing a nonprofit, consumer-oriented, locally owned alternative to the for-profit financial sector.

Community credit unions have a tremendous opportunity to bring credit union services to millions of consumers who have not previously had the option of joining a credit union. As with most worthwhile pursuits, however, it is neither a simple nor an easy task. Although community credit unions share many of the same characteristics as credit unions serving single or multiple groups, they have additional challenges and more complex decision making. This handbook does not pretend to have all of the answers. Rather, it is designed to help credit unions understand the challenges they face and suggest ways to meet them.

> *Community credit unions have a tremendous opportunity to bring credit union services to millions of consumers who have not previously had the option of joining a credit union.*

This handbook begins by tracing the roots of community credit unions from their origins in nineteenth-century Europe and explains why the occupational common bond gained favor during the heyday of credit union organization. Chapter 2 describes the changes brought about by the passage of H.R. 1151; chapter 3 makes the case for serving the entire community. You'll learn the importance of image in chapter 4. In chapter 5, the elements of an effective community relations program are described, and chapter 6 details the issues that an occupational charter faces in converting to a community charter. Sorting out the role of technology versus brick-and-mortar branches is the focus of chapter 7. The critical role of mortgages and business lending in the product mix is described in chapter 8. Finally, chapter 9 provides a brief regulatory overview. Additional information is available from the sources cited in "Resources," at the back of the book.

In 1938, Roy Bergengren, the credit union pioneer whose work is described briefly in chapter 1, spoke of the "place of the credit union in the changing picture." "Nothing stands still," he said. "We go forward with the relentless onward surge of the human race, or we go backward. We must be receptive to new ideas within the credit union movement. What, after all, is our objective? To help our people to advance steadily to a better economic lot."

"The purpose of the organization is simply the maximum service to the membership," Bergengren added. "We exist solely for service; let that burn itself into your very soul."

We exist solely for service; let that burn itself into your very soul.

Those words, spoken as the nation was slowly climbing out of the depths of the Great Depression, ring as true today when credit unions, particularly community credit unions, have the potential to grow much more quickly in the new millennium. That opportunity to serve more people would no doubt please Bergengren and the many other pioneers in whose footsteps modern credit union leaders follow.

BACK TO THE FUTURE

Learner Objectives

Upon completion of this chapter, you will be able to

1. explain the historic significance of community credit unions;

2. identify why credit unions in the United States were organized primarily around occupational groups; and

3. cite the regulatory decisions leading up to passage of H.R. 1151, the Credit Union Membership Access Act.

Credit union critics contend that credit unions act like banks but do so without bank charters. They are particularly vocal about community credit unions. They often cite the "duck" argument, which goes like this: Credit unions act like ducks, they quack like ducks, but they don't pay taxes like ducks do. What these critics fail to note are the fundamental differences between ducks and credit unions. A brief look at the historical underpinnings of the credit union movement in figure 1.1 explains those differences.

BORN IN DESPERATE TIMES

The roots of the cooperative credit movement were put down during a time of widespread suffering. It was nineteenth-century Europe, and nationalist revolutions

Figure 1.1 Credit Union Historical Time Line

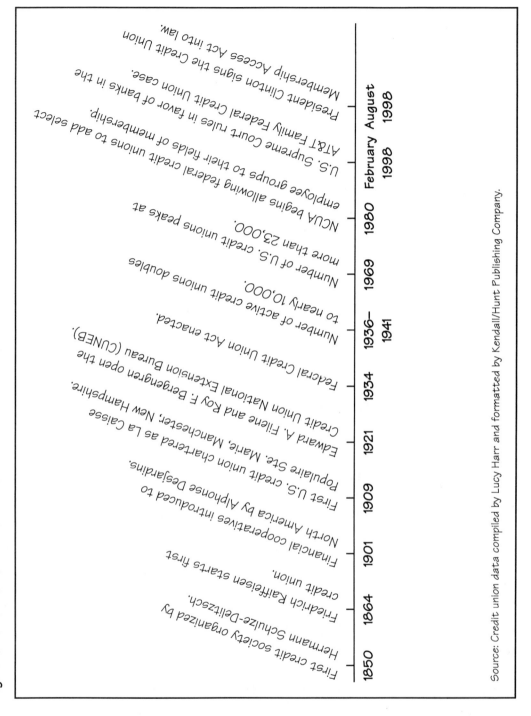

1850	1864	1901	1909	1921	1934	1936–1941	1969	1980	February 1998 / August 1998

First credit society organized by Hermann Schulze-Delitzsch.

Friedrich Raiffeisen starts first credit union.

Financial cooperatives introduced to North America by Alphonse Desjardins.

First U.S. credit union chartered as La Caisse Populaire Ste. Marie, Manchester, New Hampshire.

Edward A. Filene and Roy F. Bergengren open the Credit Union National Extension Bureau (CUNEB).

Federal Credit Union Act enacted.

Number of active credit unions doubles to nearly 10,000.

Number of U.S. credit unions peaks at more than 23,000.

NCUA begins allowing federal credit unions to add select employee groups to their fields of membership.

U.S. Supreme Court rules in favor of banks in the AT&T Family Federal Credit Union case.

President Clinton signs the Credit Union Membership Access Act into law.

Source: Credit union data compiled by Lucy Harr and formatted by Kendall/Hunt Publishing Company.

and workers' uprisings swept the continent, while economic depression and famine caused far-reaching misery. Neither government aid programs nor charity provided relief. Slowly, people realized that if they were to survive economically they would need to work together; the idea of a cooperative—mutual self-help—began to take hold.

The first credit society was organized in 1850 by civil servant Hermann Schulze-Delitzsch. Anyone willing to accept the requirements could belong.

The first credit society was organized in 1850 by civil servant Hermann Schulze-Delitzsch. Anyone willing to accept the requirements could belong. Members paid an entrance fee to help cover administrative costs, and contributed to the organization's capital by buying at least one share, which could be paid in installments. To encourage saving and procure funds for loans, deposits earned dividends. Loans were granted based on character. Loan rates were reasonable. Each member had one vote, regardless of shares, and participated in running the society through elected committees. These credit societies served a large, mixed membership drawn from a wide area.

The credit union idea spread from the cities to the countryside. Friedrich Raiffeisen, mayor of a rural district in Bavaria, came to see cooperative credit as a way to address economic and social ills. He started his first credit union in 1864 using the ideas and operating principles that had already proven effective: democratic control, equal rights of members, volunteer operation, and minimum participation levels. Typically, these credit unions served inhabitants of a single, small village.

The number of financial cooperatives increased slowly at first, then more rapidly. The cooperative idea spread throughout Europe, and in 1901 was introduced to North America by Alphonse Desjardins, who had studied the European concepts. Desjardins, a journalist who decided people needed an alternative to loan sharks and pawn shops, organized La Caisse Populaire de Lévis with a group of his neighbors. It began operation out of Desjardins's home in Lévis, Quebec, as the first credit union in North America.

From Parish to Community

In the United States, the development of credit unions came from several sources. Edward A. Filene, a Boston merchant and philanthropist, learned about cooperative credit during his travels to India. Alphonse Desjardins's work in Canada inspired leaders in Manchester, New Hampshire, where the first U.S. credit union was chartered. The parishioners of St. Mary's Church in Manchester, New Hampshire, decided they wanted to form a credit union and invited Desjardins to help them. The first U.S. credit union was organized in 1908 and chartered in 1909. Called La Caisse Populaire Ste. Marie, it was chartered under a special act of the New Hampshire legislature. The Caisse Populaire Ste. Marie is known today as St. Mary's Bank, a community credit union that is still in operation and continues its progressive tradition.

Growth came slowly at first because no one was spending enough time and effort to organize credit unions. But monetary support from the philanthropist Filene and the organizing abilities of Roy F. Bergengren, a Massachusetts attorney hired by Filene, eventually fostered the growth of U.S. credit unions. Filene spent more than a million dollars of his own money to develop U.S. credit unions.

An Expedient Route

In July 1921, the two men opened the Credit Union National Extension Bureau (CUNEB). For the next thirteen years, Bergengren spoke to state and federal legislators about the need for credit unions among the American people. Faced with the daunting task of organizing hundreds of credit unions, Bergengren realized the expediency of working through employers. He spoke to company officials and employee groups about the advantages they would enjoy if they set up credit unions for themselves. Little by little, state by state, laws were enacted, credit unions were organized, and leagues were formed.

In 1934, the Federal Credit Union Act was enacted. With a dual chartering system in place, credit unions blossomed. Between 1936 and 1941, the number of active credit unions nearly doubled, to almost 10,000. Although World War II forced the liquidation of many small credit unions (the number dropped to 8,500 by 1945), post-war prosperity provided fertile ground for credit union growth.

The number of credit unions peaked in 1969 when there were more than 23,000 credit unions in operation. Most had fields of membership based on a single common bond, an employer group, following the precedent set by Bergengren's successful organizational efforts. Bergengren was a pragmatic man. Not only was it more efficient to organize groups in the workplace, it was an effective risk management strategy. Credit unions were run primarily by volunteers and without the advantages of computers and electronic credit reports. But a credit union with a closed common bond was largely protected from overwhelming accounting problems and excess losses.

It was more efficient to organize groups in the workplace and it was an effective risk-management strategy.

Louise McCarren Herring, the "mother of Ohio credit unions," in an essay in *Sharing the American Dream,* noted that in the 1930s, "there was no data processing and only a few mechanical bookkeeping machines. As a result, [credit union] leaders felt the ideal credit union should consist of no more than 300–500 potential members. When we attempted to organize credit unions in large corporations, for instance, we organized enough groups so that the limit of membership in each group would be approximately 300 to 500. Often we organized more than one credit union per floor of a large corporation. Thus, the volunteer treasurer, or even a paid one, could keep the records up to date and service the member."

Limitations on memberships also made the passage of the Federal Credit Union Act more palatable to legislators, who then, as now, were lobbied by bankers and banker groups.

But economic conditions in the 1980s forced a change in the federal regulator's field of membership policies. The National Credit Union Administration (NCUA) began allowing federal credit unions to add select employee groups to their fields of membership. NCUA's interpretation of the Federal Credit Union Act was that multiple groups were permitted, provided each group had a common bond. This allowed credit unions to diversify their membership bases, and thus strengthen their financial condition. This was particularly important for military credit unions subject to base closings, as well as to credit unions serving "rust belt" industries. The policy also allowed businesses that were too small to support a credit union of their own access to credit union services for their employees. In 1990, that policy was challenged in the courts by the bankers and their trade groups. In a case involving AT&T Family Federal Credit Union that went all the way to the Supreme Court, the bankers prevailed in a 5–4 decision handed down in February 1998.

Because only Congress could ultimately settle the field of membership question, legislation was introduced in March 1997 clarifying that NCUA could determine what groups could belong to a credit union. The loss in the courts made passage of that legislation—the Credit Union Membership Access Act—imperative. A massive grassroots lobbying effort swung into action, and on August 7, 1998, President Bill Clinton signed the bill into law. The law generally allows federal credit unions to sign up groups of fewer than 3,000 employees. The law affects virtually all credit unions because it sets limits on member business loans and establishes statutory capital standards.

CREDIT UNIONS TODAY

Today, there are fewer than half the number of credit unions than 1969's peak of 23,000, and the majority of credit unions serve members from more than one employer. Community credit unions are the fastest-growing segment of the industry, as a record number of credit unions have applied to change their charters to community charters. As noted in figure 1.2, from 1990 to 1999 the number of credit unions continued to decline, but the number of community credit unions jumped 16 percent.

Figure 1.2 Community Credit Unions by the Numbers

	1990	Mid-1999
Number of credit unions	14,549	11,224
Number of community credit unions	913	1,059
Percentage of community credit unions to all credit unions	6.2%	9.4%
Percent decrease in number of credit unions since 1990:	−23%	
Percent increase in number of community credit unions:	16%	

"Ducks" and Credit Unions

Community credit unions' role in the history of credit unions provides strong evidence that credit unions are different from other financial institutions, not because of limited fields of membership, but because they are not-for-profit, democratically controlled, and directed by volunteers. The passage of the Credit Union Membership Access Act marked a major milestone, not only because it reaffirmed the right of NCUA—not banks or banking groups—to decide field of membership issues, but because it allows significant groups of consumers the chance to participate in a credit union. Chapter 2 provides details on how the act affected community credit union charters.

THE NEW RULES

Learner Objectives

Upon completion of this chapter, you will be able to

1. identify NCUA requirements for community charters under IRPS-99;

2. describe those individuals eligible for membership based on their relationship to the community or to an existing member;

3. list the special requirements for serving the underserved; and

4. explain the characteristics of community development credit unions.

Passage of the Credit Union Membership Access Act in August, 1998, was a historic victory for U.S. credit unions, a cause for celebration throughout the movement. On a practical level, however, it meant that federal credit unions seeking to expand would need to abide by new rules. Previously, field of membership policies established in NCUA's Interpretive Ruling and Policy Statement 94-1 applied. Now, IRPS-99, the Field of Membership and Chartering Manual, dated January 1, 1999, is in effect. State-chartered credit unions continue to follow the rules established by their respective states. Although some states mirror the federal rules, others are more or less restrictive.

Community Charters Under IRPS-99

NCUA requires community charters for federal credit unions to be based on a single, well-defined local community, neighborhood, or rural district where individuals have common interests or interact. Under prior NCUA policy, a credit union applying for a community charter had to demonstrate sufficient interaction among persons in the community to qualify. The new policy includes an alternate standard of having "common interests." Now the credit union applicant must prove that the individuals in the geographic area interact *or* that they have common interests. Either or both is sufficient.

The word "local" was added by Congress and was intended to be more limiting than previous policies.

The community also must meet the criteria of a *local* community, neighborhood, or rural district. The word *local* was added by Congress and was intended to be more limiting than previous policies. Most notable is the requirement that the residents of the proposed community area interact or have common interests, which is determined by a number of factors. According to NCUA, the existence of a single major trade area, shared municipal or recreational facilities, or an area newspaper may be sufficient evidence of community interaction and/or common interests. On the other hand, numerous trade areas, multiple taxing authorities, or multiple political jurisdictions tend to weaken the case.

Population and geography are also significant in determining whether the area is local. A large population in a small geographic area or a small population in a large geographic area may meet NCUA community chartering requirements. But a larger population in a larger geographic area may not. Clearly, it's harder for a major metropolitan city, a densely populated county, or an area covering several counties with a large population to have sufficient interaction and/or common interests, and therefore it's harder to show that these areas meet the local requirement. In such cases, NCUA requires more evidence of interaction and/or common interests than is required for a smaller area.

NCUA will usually consider the community requirements to be met when the area to be served comprises:

- a recognized single political jurisdiction not greater than a county or its equivalent, or two or more contiguous political jurisdictions wholly contained within a single county or its equivalent, and with a population at or below 300,000;
- multiple contiguous political jurisdictions exceeding the boundaries of a single county or its equivalent, and with a population at or below 200,000.

If the area to be served meets one of those criteria, the credit union can submit a narrative of how the area meets the standards for community interaction or common interests. This includes describing, in detail, the community's trade areas, shared facilities, organizations, media, and so forth. Three other items are required: maps depicting the boundaries and surrounding areas, business and marketing plans showing the credit union can adequately serve the community, and evidence of the population. If these materials fail to convince NCUA that community interaction or a set of common interests exists, then more detailed documentation is needed. NCUA's regional offices also may request additional information in support of the application. Figure 2.1 lists examples of acceptable documentation under IRPS-99.

It's possible for more than one credit union to serve a community, but once a credit union converts from a single common bond or multiple common bond to a community charter, it can no longer serve people within those groups who don't otherwise qualify by living, working, worshiping, or attending school in the service area. Members of record can continue to belong. The credit union must notify the groups that will no longer be served.

Community credit unions come in all sizes. While most are between $20 and $50 million in assets—some 215 at mid-year 1999—there are sixty-six with less than $500,000 in assets, and seven with $500 million or more. Figure 2.2 shows the distribution of assets along the asset continuum.

ALL IN THE FAMILY

If a federal credit union so desires, the rules also allow membership to a number of people with close relationships to the community. These include

- spouses of persons who died while within the field of membership of this credit union;

Figure 2.1 Acceptable Documentation Under IRPS-99

- The defined political jurisdictions.
- Major trade areas (shopping patterns and traffic flows).
- Shared/common facilities (for example, educational, medical, police and fire protection, school district, water, and others).
- Organizations and clubs within the community area.
- Newspapers or other periodicals published for and about the area.
- Maps designating the area to be served. (One map must be a regional or state map with the proposed community outlined. The other must outline the proposed community and the identifying geographic characteristics of the surrounding areas.)
- Common characteristics and background of residents (for example, income, religious beliefs, primary ethnic groups, similarity of occupations, household types, primary age group, and others).
- Other documentation that demonstrates the area is a community where individuals have common interests or interact.

- employees of this credit union;
- volunteers in the community;
- members of the immediate family or household; and
- organizations of such persons.

Previously, federal credit unions could define "immediate family" in any way they wanted, but the new rules provide specific guidelines.

Previously, federal credit unions could define "immediate family" in any way they wanted, but the new rules provide specific guidelines. Immediate family is defined as spouse, child, sibling, parent, grandparent, or grandchild and includes stepparents, stepchildren, stepsiblings, and adoptive relationships. "Household" is defined as persons living in the same residence maintaining a single economic

---

Figure 2.2 Distribution of Asset Size Among Community Credit Unions

By Asset Size ($ in millions)	Number of Community Credit Unions
0.0–0.5	66
0.5–1.0	49
1.0–2.0	60
2.0–5.0	112
5.0–10.0	133
10.0–20.0	180
20.0–50.0	215
50.0–100.0	127
100.0–200.0	67
200.0–500.0	43
500.0 and over	7
Total	1,059

Source: NCUA June 1999 Call Report Data.

unit. That means a domestic partner of a primary member would qualify for membership, but college roommates who share only living space would not. The primary member must be eligible to join the credit union, but doesn't actually have to be a member for his or her immediate family or household member to join, provided the immediate family or household clause is included in the field of membership. However, it is necessary for the immediate family member or household member to join first for that person's immediate family member or household member to join the credit union. A credit union can adopt a more restrictive definition of immediate family or household.

Here's an example: Mary lives in California. Her brother John and his family live in Metropolis, Florida. The XYZ Federal Credit Union serves a field of membership that includes John's residence and has a family membership clause that includes siblings. John doesn't belong to XYZ Federal Credit Union, but Mary, who's fed up with paying high service fees at her local financial institution, reads about the great rates and services at XYZ in a newspaper advertisement and decides to join. She recognizes that having a debit and a credit card, Internet access to XYZ FCU's web site and the credit union's toll-free audio response system will make it relatively easy to belong.

Even though brother John—the person eligible for primary membership—is not taking advantage of the benefits of membership, Mary can. On the other hand, if it were Mary's husband, Bill, who recognized the advantages of joining and wants to do so, he can't unless Mary joins first. Once Mary joins, however, he can, too. (John finally sees the light and joins XYZ once he hears Mary, then Bill, extol the virtues of the credit union. Marketing tip: Never underestimate the power of word-of-mouth marketing.)

Under the Federal Credit Union Act, once a person becomes a member of the credit union, he or she may remain a member until choosing to withdraw or in the rare event of expulsion from the membership—the "once a member, always a member" provision. However, a credit union may restrict services to members who are no longer within the field of membership.

SERVING THE UNDERSERVED

Credit unions serve both an economic and a social purpose.

Credit unions were created to fill an unmet need: to provide "people of modest means" both a place to save and borrow, and the opportunity to learn money management skills. Credit unions serve both an economic and social purpose. To encourage credit unions to reach out to those most in need of financial services, any federally chartered credit union, including a community credit union, may include in its field of membership, without regard to location, communities that meet the definition of an underserved area. The credit union must meet three minimum requirements:

- Establish that the area is a community.
- Develop a business plan on how it will serve that community.
- Put a facility in the community.

There are specifics about what constitutes an "underserved area." According to NCUA, an underserved area is a well-defined local community, neighborhood, or rural district that is an "investment area" as defined in section 103(16) of the Community Development Banking and Financial Institutions Act of 1994. Figure 2.3 lists areas defined as underserved.

Figure 2.3 Underserved Areas

- An area encompassed or located in an Empowerment Zone or Enterprise Community designated under section 1391 of the Internal Revenue Code of 1996 (26 U.S.C. 1391).
- An area where the percentage of the population living in poverty is at least 20 percent, and the area has significant unmet needs for loans or equity investments.
- An area in a Metropolitan Area, where the median family income is at or below 80 percent of the Metropolitan Area median family income or the national Metropolitan Area median family income, whichever is greater; and the area has significant unmet needs for loans or equity investments.
- An area outside of a Metropolitan Area, where the median family income is at or below 80 percent of the statewide non-Metropolitan Area median family income or the national non-Metropolitan Area median family income, whichever is greater; and the area has significant unmet needs for loans or equity investments.
- An area where the unemployment rate is at least 1.5 times the national average, and the area has significant unmet needs for loans or equity investments.
- An area where the percentage of occupied distressed housing (as indicated by lack of complete plumbing and occupancy of more than one person per room) is at least 20 percent, and the area has significant unmet needs for loans or equity investments.
- An area located outside of a Metropolitan Area with a county population loss between 1980 and 1990 of at least 10 percent, and the area has significant unmet needs for loans or equity investments.

A "metropolitan area" has a specific meaning. The Office of Management and Budget defines metropolitan areas for purposes of collecting, tabulating, and publishing federal data. Metropolitan area definitions result from applying published standards to Census Bureau data. Metropolitan areas are a large population nucleus, together with adjacent communities having a high degree of social and economic integration with that core. Metropolitan areas make up one or more entire counties, except in New England, where cities and towns are the basic geographic units. They are defined each year, with the data released in June.

"Significant unmet needs for loans or equity investments" can be determined by studies or analyses such as Home Mortgage Disclosure Act (HMDA) data about the availability of mortgage financing, demographics of financial institutions in the area, Community Reinvestment Act (CRA) ratings of those institutions located in the targeted area, or statistics from the local Chamber of Commerce documenting a lack of business development.

As noted earlier, credit unions seeking approval to serve an underserved area must first establish that the area is a community and develop a business plan. The plan must identify the community's credit and depository needs and explain the strategies for serving them. The credit union also must maintain an office or facility in the community. For underserved areas, a service facility is defined as a place where shares and loan applications are accepted and loans are disbursed. This includes a credit-union-owned branch, a shared branch, a mobile branch, or a credit-union-owned electronic facility that meets, at a minimum, these requirements. An office open on a regularly scheduled weekly basis and a mobile branch that goes to the same location weekly also qualify. However, an automated teller machine (ATM) does not meet the facility definition.

For many credit unions, these requirements may seem too burdensome. In chapter 3, we'll profile some credit unions that have succeeded in reaching out to low-income communities.

COMMUNITY DEVELOPMENT CREDIT UNIONS

Credit unions established to serve primarily low-income areas are called community development credit unions. To qualify for the below market-rate loans and technical assistance grants provided through the National Credit Union Administration's Revolving Loan Program and to be able to accept nonmember deposits, community development credit unions must apply for and receive a special low-income designation. There are approximately 1,500 community development federally insured credit unions, although the majority have not applied for the low-income designation.

To secure the low-income designation, a credit union must show that a majority of its member households earn less than 80 percent of the national median household income.

Low-income credit unions often need third-party deposits, low-interest loans, and technical assistance to enable them to grow and stabilize their operations. Only LICU-designated credit unions are allowed to accept nonmember deposits from any source—usually from larger credit unions, banks seeking Community Reinvestment Act credit, foundations, faith-based institutions, and other social investors.

Typically, a credit union uses the below-market-rate loans from the Revolving Loan Program to meet loan demand from its members, while grants usually are used to purchase office equipment, provide salary assistance to hire qualified managers or train staffers and volunteers, and secure professional audits of financial records. NCUA's Office of Community Development Credit Unions provides counseling and administers the loan program.

REACHING OUT

The objective of the Credit Union Membership Access Act is to provide more people the opportunity to join a credit union. To accomplish this, NCUA has streamlined procedures for federal credit unions seeking a community charter. Those meeting the criteria are able to reach out to people who previously did not have access. State-chartered credit unions continue to follow the rules in their respective states.

COMMUNITY CREDIT UNIONS, CREDIT UNION PHILOSOPHY, AND GOOD BUSINESS

Learner Objectives

Upon completion of this chapter, you will be able to

1. identify the competitive challenges community credit unions face;

2. describe the special strategies necessary to serve the entire community, including the underserved; and

3. evaluate all policies in light of their effect on the entire membership.

Credit unions have a rich history of providing financial services in a way that puts service and benefits to members above all else. The long-standing credit union motto, "Not for profit, not for charity, but for service," guides the policies of thousands of credit unions—large and small; single sponsor and community; those that are "plain vanilla," providing just loans and shares; and those that are full service. Every credit union puts its "people helping people" philosophy into action in a different way. The challenge for the community credit union is to adopt business development strategies that are consistent with credit union philosophy, and at the same time, to operate in a safe and sound manner. Although profit is not the prime motivator, a credit union still must have net income if it is to continue to exist.

Every credit union puts its "people helping people" philosophy into action in a different way.

Two other factors come into play. Frequently, community credit unions must compete head-to-head with other local financial institutions, and secondly, they often do not have meaningful support from a sponsor. As a result, a community credit union often faces financial and operational issues that differ from those encountered by an occupational or associational credit union.

SPECIAL CHALLENGES

Many single sponsor credit unions may pay little, if any, rent, for example, and can rely heavily on word-of-mouth advertising. Any marketing they do is to a more homogeneous group than is found in the general population. According to Raddon Financial Group, community credit unions spend more marketing dollars per member than average, yet they are the least efficient type of credit union. Community credit unions cannot use a "one-size-fits-all" marketing approach successfully. It is doomed to fail because a diverse membership requires marketing programs targeted to different segments of the community. And while a community credit union can use mass media, such as newspapers, radio, and television, more effectively to promote its services than can a single associational or occupational credit union, the message still needs to be tailored to the target audience.

A lack of payroll deduction requires alternative strategies for promoting savings programs. It may also affect the collections staff at a community credit union, who must find alternative ways to promote regular, on-time payments on loans. Accordingly, a credit union applying for a federal community charter must develop a detailed and practical business and marketing plan for at least the first two years of operation. State-chartered credit unions may have to provide a similar document.

According to NCUA, the proposed credit union not only must address the documentation requirements described earlier, but also must focus on the "accomplishment of the unique financial and operational factors of a community charter."

"Community credit unions will be expected to regularly review and to follow, to the fullest extent economically possible, the marketing and business plan submitted with their application," the agency notes. Credit unions applying for a state charter to serve a community may face similar requirements.

SERVING THE ENTIRE COMMUNITY

Even if your credit union has not amended or does not plan to amend its charter to specifically include a low-income community, chances are there are people who meet a practical definition of low income who reside within your field of membership. For example, there may be seniors who have assets, but who live on a low, fixed income. They may be students. They may be single-parent families. They may be the working poor, even families with two wage earners, but who labor for minimum wage and have high child care expenses. As the statistics in figure 3.1 show, household median income varies considerably depending on a household's characteristics.

Policy Roadblocks

Whatever the circumstances, it's prudent to examine your credit union's policies to ensure that you are not unwittingly disenfranchising potential members. Then it's critical to adopt new or revised policies if necessary. Anecdotal evidence suggests that credit unions sometimes encounter difficulties with their examinations because of their attempts to serve the underserved. In some cases, however, it's because they are in violation of their own policies.

Check Verification System

If your policies require use of a check verification system to screen new members, you may be automatically pushing away those with modest incomes, who may have, at some point, written checks on nonsufficient funds. You may need to establish an exception policy in which members who've previously bounced checks are allowed to open a share account and use money orders, rather than a traditional share draft account.

Another strategy employed by some credit unions is to issue a debit card that allows access to cash via ATMs and that can be used for point-of-sale transactions. Money orders also can be made available; sometimes a limited number are provided free each month. Some credit unions offer educational sessions to teach

Figure 3.1 Household Composition and Median Income

Households	Median Income (1998)
All households	$38,885
Age of householder	
15 to 24 years	$23,564
25 to 34 years	$40,069
35 to 44 years	$48,451
45 to 54 years	$54,148
55 to 64 years	$43,167
65 years and older	$21,729
Family households	
Married couple	$54,276
Female, no husband present	$24,393
Male, no wife present	$39,414
Race and ethnic origin	
White	$40,912
Black	$25,351
Asian/Pacific Islander	$46,637
Hispanic origin	$28,330
Residence	
Inside metropolitan areas	$40,983
Inside central cities	$33,151
Outside central cities	$46,402
Outside metropolitan areas	$32,022

Source: U.S. Census Bureau

members checking account management skills. Then the credit unions provide a share draft account on a probationary basis.

Deposits or Balances

Other potential roadblocks for modest income people are minimum opening deposits or minimum account balances that they perceive to be out of reach. The Consumer Federation of America estimates that some 12 million households do not have bank accounts through which to deposit checks and pay bills. They rely on the "fringe bankers" or the alternative financial sector (AFS)—check-cashing outlets, rent-to-own, and pawn shops—to meet their financial services needs.

"Most people turn to the AFS because their financial characteristics exclude them from the services of deposit institutions," John Caskey argues in his Filene Research Institute report *Lower Income Americans, Higher Cost Financial Services.* Caskey, associate professor at Swarthmore College and the nation's leading expert on the AFS, also found that some AFS customers could use banks or credit unions, but choose AFS businesses for their unique services, and perhaps, because they don't realize the extent of the cost differential. The result is that people least able to afford it, pay more—sometimes significantly more—for financial services. Because people with modest incomes tend to have what Caskey describes as a "cash and carry" lifestyle—they cash their paychecks, use money orders to pay bills, and then carry what remains as cash—they are never able to accumulate savings and thus, never move away from living on the edge.

Betty Matthiessen, a credit union consultant with extensive experience working with low-income populations, suggests allowing installment payments for minimum deposits. Florida Central Credit Union in Tampa, Florida, for example, requires a minimum deposit of $50, but allows a member to meet it through a series of small deposits over a ninety-day period.

English As a Second Language

Another issue is serving segments of the community for whom English is a second language. At a minimum, this can be a labor-intensive process. Recognize that tellers or member service representatives may need to spend more time than average to explain and process transactions. All-out marketing efforts require not only translation of materials, but also an understanding of any relevant cultural issues.

RETHINKING THE SERVICE PACKAGE

Not all markets within a community credit union's field of membership need or use the same set of financial services, either. A service menu that includes credit cards with high limits, jumbo mortgages, and boat loans for more affluent members also may need to include convenient check cashing and a way to pay bills not requiring checking accounts for members at the other end of the income scale. You may need to rethink your service packages, too. For example, Professor Caskey believes that "lifeline banking" proposals that require a checking account are misguided. These lifeline banking proposals surface periodically in both state legislatures and in Congress and are meant to guarantee access to financial services. They are modeled after the "lifeline energy" laws that prevent utilities from shutting off heat in the winter in cold climates and air conditioning in the summer in warm ones. But checking accounts with low balances—the likely scenario for modest-income families—invite bounced checks. A money order program is far more practical.

Savings programs, while important for members of all income levels, are critical for those with low incomes. According to the Filene Research Institute study cited earlier, the primary reason low-income households do not have a deposit account in a bank, savings and loan, or credit union, is because they have no, or very little, savings. This makes it difficult to cope with even minor financial crises. By encouraging savings, credit unions can change lives dramatically and free many from the need to patronize high-cost AFS lenders, according to the Filene study.

Containing Costs

Credit unions seeking to reach out to lower-income members may be concerned about the high cost of doing so.

Credit unions seeking to reach out to lower-income members may be concerned about the high cost of doing so. And rightly so. A 1999 Filene Research Institute report, *Credit Unions and Asset Accumulation by Lower-Income Households,* by John Caskey and David B. Humphrey, notes that the following characteristics of lower-income households can drive up service costs:

- Low balances; any funds deposited are withdrawn within a few days,
- Reluctance to use automated means to transfer funds, make deposits, or verify account balances,
- Frequent teller visits to verify balances or purchase money orders, and
- Living paycheck to paycheck without a financial safety margin, which often means missed payments for rent, utilities, or debt service, resulting in impaired credit. Thus, there's no loan revenue to offset deposit costs.

Efforts to overcome these obstacles—for example, extensive educational initiatives or incentives to promote long-term savings—also will increase costs. Caskey and Humphrey offer three broad categories of strategies to contain costs.

First, *cross-subsidize*. Support efforts targeted at lower-income members with earnings from the general membership. The smaller the subsidy, the greater chance of success. On a large scale, using this strategy may raise fairness issues.

Second, *impose fees*. Charge for specific services to cover their cost. Although this strategy is not viable for basic financial education or to provide incentives for savings, it may work for transaction services. Chances are, the rates will be lower than at the other available alternative, commercial check-cashing outlets. Similarly, charging higher interest rates on higher-risk loans offers an alternative to consumer finance companies and payday loan shops.

Third, *lower or share costs*. Look for ways to lower costs. A number of credit unions have found they can serve underserved populations by forming a partnership with another organization that is willing to absorb or pay expenses. The Over-the-Rhine branch of Cincinnati Central Credit Union, for example, serves a low-income population by partnering with a nonprofit organization called SmartMoney Community Services. While the specific details of the partnership have evolved since initial meetings in 1986, the basic elements have remained the same: The credit union provides the residents of the community with low-cost financial services, and SmartMoney provides financial education, subsidizes office space, and serves as a link to the community, helping to build trust between the residents and the credit union. Others have encouraged automated ways to access credit union services to cut transaction costs.

Accepting the Challenge

The Filene study also cites the example of Citizens Equity Federal Credit Union (CEFCU), a $1.8 billion community-based credit union serving more than 200,000 members in Peoria, Illinois, and in some other cities and towns in Illinois. CEFCU opened a branch in a low-income community in Peoria that had no other deposit institutions. Two-thirds of the residents live in households with incomes below the federal poverty line. CEFCU accepted the challenge of providing financial services to the area—called Valley Park—when a local developer rehabilitated a strip mall with help from public funding incentives. The credit union located the branch inside the mall's anchor tenant, a high-traffic convenience store/gas station. This increased its security as well as its members' perception of security.

Because some 60 percent of the area's households already included a CEFCU member, the new branch was well received. CEFCU also made efforts to become part of the community by contributing money and volunteers to various nonprofit agencies. The credit union has successfully reduced the demand for teller services by installing an automated teller machine inside the branch. The "Fast-Track Teller" ATM can cash checks to the penny and members who sign up for the service can use the ATM to pay electric and gas bills electronically. Members also can allocate deposits to different accounts.

CEFCU promotes savings in two important ways. Although the credit union has an account maintenance fee for members who do not use enough services or do not maintain sufficient deposits or loan balances, this fee is waived for members in households with incomes under $30,000 or for members 25 or younger or older than 62. This is a credit-union-wide policy, but one that is particularly beneficial to members using this branch.

The branch staff also provide extensive informal financial counseling to members by encouraging the use of savings accounts and discouraging the use of rent-to-own and payday lending operations. They also help members understand credit reports and discuss steps to take to improve their credit profiles.

LENDING POLICIES

Credit unions seeking to serve the entire community must face the fundamental issue of how they will extend credit to people of "modest means," as well as to people with "less than modest means." Some credit unions, including community credit unions, have found that pricing loans based on the borrower's creditworthiness allows them to provide loans to a wider spectrum of members. Charging consumers with a blemished credit record higher rates has been a long-standing practice of banks and is the fundamental business strategy employed by finance companies. This, in itself, makes some credit unions reluctant to implement a risk-based lending or risk-based pricing plan. They are also concerned about the disproportionate effect such pricing has on low-income members. "The poor pay more" clashes with their underlying credit union values.

On the other hand, denying a large percentage of loan applications from low-income members leaves them with the unsavory alternative of dealing with higher-cost lenders, such as pawn shops, finance companies, or auto title operations. These members are perhaps better served by raising interest rates to reflect the extra risk involved. Even if they pay the highest rate allowed at federal credit unions—18 percent APR—they will pay considerably less than the 25 percent, or 36 percent, or more routinely charged by the other sources of credit available to them.

Betty Matthiessen notes that loan minimums also may put the credit union out of reach for some members of the community. "If your loan minimum is $1,500, it's likely that some won't qualify for it. Plus, they only need $400," she says. And while many people could use their credit card for these smaller loan amounts, many low-income people don't qualify or don't have a credit card. The Filene study *Lower Income Americans, Higher Cost Financial Services,* points out that credit unions seeking to serve lower-income members need to recognize the market for the quick availability of micro-loans between $50 and $300. If your loan policies require higher minimum amounts, you may be unable to serve the people who need the credit union the most.

Matthiessen recognizes that many credit unions feel they can't make small loans because they are "not profitable"—they lose money on them. She recommends looking for ways to make them feasible, if not profitable, including streamlining procedures to eliminate as many labor-intensive steps as possible. This might include using preprinted forms with a standard loan amount, for example, similar to the holiday loans offered by many credit unions. Open-end lending plans can significantly reduce the paperwork involved in granting credit. See chapter 8 for more information.

Open-end lending plans can significantly reduce the paperwork involved in granting credit.

Maria Berkowitz, branch manager at Central Appalachia People's Federal Credit Union (CAPFCU) in Berea, Kentucky, points out that medical bills are often the source of blemishes on credit records for people with limited resources, who have minimal or no health insurance. When the bills become delinquent, the hospital or clinic may turn them over to a collection agency, but collection is not pursued aggressively. Berkowitz notes that these bills then become a case of "out of sight, out of mind." The unpaid bills, however, do turn up on credit reports. So, for example, if your credit union has a loan policy in place that requires a spot-free credit report to qualify for a mortgage, you will not be able to serve the entire community. At CAPFCU, rather than automatically turning down a mortgage for members with these types of bills, the credit union works with them to clear up the debt so they can qualify for the loan.

POLICIES AND VALUES WORKING TOGETHER

Your credit union's policies reflect your credit union's fundamental values. Obviously, they must comply with government rules and regulations. But beyond that, they must allow you to meet the financial needs of your entire community in a way that puts the credit union motto of "Not for profit, not for charity, but for service" into practice. That will require careful thought and analysis. As many great philosophers have noted, although things can be made simple, they cannot be made easy.

BUILDING YOUR IMAGE

Learner Objectives

Upon completion of this chapter, you will be able to

1. explain why image is important;

2. identify the elements of a corporate identity program;

3. name a credit union's stakeholders;

4. find information about your credit union's image; and

5. list the components of an image campaign.

In their entertaining book, *Do Lunch or Be Lunch, The Power of Predictability in Creating Your Future,* Harvard Business School Professor Howard H. Stevenson and communications consultant Jeffrey L. Cruikshank suggest that the reasons people join any organization are to

- engage in coordinated actions;
- move society forward; and
- make our predicted futures come true.

"We build on a collective sense of what's important in order to invest in the future," they note.

Although people who join a credit union may not be able to verbalize these goals, they may understand intuitively that a credit union provides them with the opportunity to improve their own financial well-being, while also helping others to do so. When asked why they joined, most people cite practical reasons: convenience, dividends on savings, reasonable rates on loans, and availability of payroll deduction plans.

Once they've joined, most consumers are content with their decision. For fifteen straight years, credit unions have earned the highest marks in customer satisfaction of any financial service organization in an independent poll conducted by the *American Banker,* a trade newspaper. Some three of four consumers who identify a credit union as their principal financial institution are "very satisfied," compared with less than 60 percent of customers of banks and other financial service providers. The most recent poll also indicated that consumers give credit unions higher ratings than banks on trustworthiness—a first-time achievement for credit unions.

Building and maintaining a positive image is a full-time, relentless task.

These ratings speak to the overall positive reputation that credit unions have worked hard to achieve. The credit union "white hat" image has reaped many rewards. Every year memberships, assets, and loans reach new levels. But anyone who has ever owned a white sofa, white wool suit, or white fedora knows that it's not easy to keep it that way. There are seemingly endless ways to cause harm: red wine, children's sticky fingers, leaky pens. For credit unions seeking to build and maintain a positive image, the "red wine" may be a disgruntled member turned down for a loan, the "sticky fingers" may be a branch manager charged with embezzlement, and the "leaky pen" may be damaging Home Mortgage Disclosure Act (HMDA) data. Building and maintaining a positive image is a full-time, relentless task. It's not easy, and it's not fast. But it's essential to your credit union's success.

WHY IS IMAGE IMPORTANT?

Ask anyone who's aware of the Penn Square investment debacle of the early 1980s or the Rhode Island private insurance crisis of the late 1980s if "image" is

---

important and you're likely to hear an emphatic "you bet." In general, people do business with organizations they trust, and that's especially the case when it comes to entrusting their money to a financial institution. Headline news about mismanaging investments or inadequate insurance protection has a way of making consumers uneasy about their own money. First and foremost, they want to be assured that their money is safe in the credit union.

There's no quick and easy way to create a positive image or a good reputation. But while it may take years to build a reputation, it takes only a moment to destroy one. Think of it this way: A comprehensive communications program is essential to a credit union, but it won't necessarily in and of itself, stop a run.

PERCEPTION IS REALITY

Every credit union has a number of stakeholders. Community credit unions, because of their increased exposure and visibility, tend to have more groups with an interest in them. These stakeholders have a profound impact on your success. Typically, stakeholders include the individuals listed in figure 4.1.

Your credit union means different things to different stakeholders. In one traditional parable, the six blind men describing the elephant each had a unique

Figure 4.1 Typical Credit Union Stakeholders

- Employees
- Boards of directors
- Volunteers
- Members
- Potential members
- Legislators and regulators
- Suppliers and vendors
- Community leaders and community groups
- Trade groups

perspective—from the man seizing the tail viewing it as a rope to the man touching the ear and announcing it was like a fan. Similarly, credit union employees tend to view the credit union from a different perspective than that of your regulator. How do these perspectives differ from what your members or leaders in your community see? What comes to mind when your credit union's name is mentioned to each of these groups? The sum total of their perceptions is your image. And their perceptions are reality. First impressions are important, but it takes a continued effort to maintain your image. That makes image and reputation management a full-time function and one for which time and money must be allocated.

First impressions are important, but it takes a continued effort to maintain your image.

Building the credit union's reputation as a safe and sound financial institution that provides quality service to its members starts in the board room. The board of directors must develop good policies that serve as the basis of your image. Think of image as the foundation of your credit union, and think of your policies as the steel reinforcement. If either is unsound or lacks integrity, eventually the foundation will crumble, and the rest of the credit union will tumble down after. Build all of your communication efforts on your credit union's image. Before embarking on a major loan promotion or membership marketing campaign, take time to assess your current reputation and any potential storm clouds on the horizon.

Fortunately, the information you need is readily available, and much of it at very little cost. The key is to listen to a wide spectrum of stakeholder sources.

1. Start with your employees. What are they hearing from members? From their neighbors and friends? Cultivate a culture within the credit union that encourages feedback from employees. Hold both formal and informal listening sessions or town meetings to encourage communication. MBWA—"management by walking around"—has fallen by the wayside, but the idea that you can learn a lot about your organization by getting out from behind your desk still has merit.

2. Listen to members. Do simple surveys. The fact that you are asking the questions lets your members know that you care about their opinions. Pay particular attention to disgruntled members. Do their complaints have merit?

3. What are your critics saying? The old saying that you can learn more from your enemies than from your friends applies here. Does the rhetoric from your local banker have some basis in fact? Do you have any particular vulnerabilities that you need to pay attention to?

4. Ask a professional. Over breakfast or lunch, ask a respected member of your community—attorney, accountant, business leader—what he or she has heard about the credit union, and about your competitors. Ask for the straight scoop; you're not interested in the sanitized version of the truth.

5. Ask other credit unions. Here, too, you need to get the unvarnished truth about your credit union's reputation.

6. Ask a reporter. If you have a good relationship with a reporter, you can turn the tables on occasion and ask him or her a few general questions about the financial services industry in your area that may reveal some insights.

7. Rev up the search engines. The World Wide Web can tell you almost anything you want to know about what people think about the world in general, and financial services in particular.

8. Watch behaviors. Are more members asking about mortgages, even though you haven't advertised them? Perhaps participation in the real estate association is paying off. On the other hand, have auto loans fallen off? Are members buying cars online and bypassing credit union financing? Stakeholders' actions can provide a great deal of information about their attitudes and perceptions toward your credit union.

Stakeholders' actions can provide a great deal of information about their attitudes and perceptions toward your credit union.

TAKE A PICTURE

Only by taking a snapshot of your current image can you most effectively plan and implement any communications materials, whether they are designed to build your image or to promote a specific product or service. In fact, it's possible the picture you take is not a pretty one. It's even possible your policies and practices are creating a problem with your image.

For example, if you've converted to a community charter and are not able to serve the entire community, as described in chapter 3, you are vulnerable. "Cherry picking" members is not an option. Always ask: "If people knew what we were doing, would we be able to withstand the scrutiny?" A good exercise is to ask a series of "What if . . ." questions:

- What if the number of membership applications or loans we turn down from low-income members becomes headline news?
- What if the comments we make internally about low-balance, high-transaction accounts were made public?
- What if our examiner's report was made public?
- What if our worst nightmare came true?

These are tough questions, but ones that need asking. Although a credit union tucked behind the doors of a factory is not exempt from doing the right thing, its failings are not nearly as likely to be shared with the rest of the world. The increased visibility enjoyed by a community credit union, however, means its operations are carefully observed.

IMAGE COMMUNICATIONS

Corporate America spends roughly a billion dollars every year on image advertising. They do so for a number of reasons—from repositioning a company to telling the "other side" of the story in the midst of a crisis. Figure 4.2 lists components of a corporate identity, which contributes to your image.

Image Campaign

Your credit union may consider an image campaign in a variety of circumstances. Image campaigns are effective communication tools to

- introduce a new name or redefine the credit union following a merger or charter conversion;
- create awareness and build understanding and acceptance of the credit union within the community;
- protect the interests of the credit union in the face of legislative or regulatory challenges by influencing public opinion;

Figure 4.2 Corporate Identity Components

Your corporate identity is not the same as your image or reputation, but it plays a critical role in establishing or maintaining your image. Some of the elements of your corporate identity follow. All should work in concert so that you are not sending mixed messages. (Keep this list in mind if you are planning to change your name as the result of a charter conversion, too.)

Advertising and Marketing/Sales

- Sales manual
- Uniform or dress code
- Lapel pin
- Videos and audiovisuals
- Exhibits and displays
- Radio, newspaper, and television ads
- Booklets, brochures
- Direct mail
- Newsletter
- Posters
- Bulletin board items
- Billboards
- Yellow Pages advertising
- Giveaways (key chains, pens, mugs, golf balls, etc.)
- Drive-up envelopes
- Statement stuffers
- Web site
- Telephone audio response system and message-on-hold

Architecture

- Exterior design
- Interior design
- Interior lobby
- Interior entrance
- Teller stations and queues
- Furnishings
- Landscaping
- Signage

Printed Materials

- Stationery
- Business cards
- Statements
- Invoices
- Checks/share drafts
- Plastic cards
- Loan and share documents
- News release
- Annual and quarterly reports
- Postal indicia

- position the credit union as a consumer-friendly, cooperative alternative to the for-profit financial sector;
- establish the credit union as an attractive workplace in order to bring in quality employees and retain the employees it has; or
- respond to a crisis.

Goodwill is an asset, but one that is not easily captured on a balance sheet.

Like any communications effort, the image campaign must have specific objectives. But unlike an ad campaign promoting a specific product, such as mortgages, the results of an image campaign may not be as easily measured. A loan promotion's effectiveness can be measured in dollars. An image campaign's effectiveness often can only be measured in goodwill. Goodwill is an asset, but one that is not easily captured on a balance sheet. Some would argue that it is so valuable, it's priceless. The image campaign also may serve more than one purpose. A campaign that serves to position the credit union as consumer friendly may also create awareness and build understanding and acceptance. Or the introduction of a new name also may attract new employees or new members.

A Case in Point

Tom Wanttie, marketing coordinator at Aberdeen Federal Credit Union in South Dakota, planned a seven-week ad campaign to culminate during International Credit Union Week. The campaign was designed to introduce a new community charter. It included newspaper and radio placements. Initially, the ads announced the charter change and its significance to the community. These were followed by product and service ads, an explanation of credit union philosophy, and an invitation to visit the credit union during ICU Week. The credit union offered door prizes to encourage attendance.

By introducing the credit union on a conceptual level, Wanttie set the stage for promoting the specific products and services the credit union has to offer. In planning an image campaign, assume that your audiences know very little about credit unions in general, and yours in particular. Although your staff, your board of directors and volunteers, and some of your members may fully understand what the credit union is and how it benefits its members and the community, few outside the walls of the credit union do. That means that explaining the basics of the credit union difference is essential to positioning your credit union in the minds of your stakeholders.

Sending the Message

Keep it simple. Communications research indicates that three messages are the maximum number that can be used effectively. Any more and the messages get buried in the resulting information overload. To ensure that your messages are having an impact, they need to be used repeatedly. The old advertising adage that the audience is just starting to get the message when you are virtually sick of hearing it applies here. Cutting through the clutter requires that you find different ways to keep saying the same thing.

For example, an image campaign designed to create awareness in the community might include these three messages:

- ABC Community Credit Union is a good deal for consumers because service, not profit, is the primary goal.
- ABC Community Credit Union is locally owned by its members, not by an out-of-state megabank.
- ABC Community Credit Union is for everyone who lives and works in ABC.

These three messages share some common characteristics:

1. They put the self-interest of the reader, and potential member, first. In formulating your messages, remember that people are interested in messages that affect them personally.
2. They are clear and direct.
3. They inform.

Of course, to get these messages across, you may say them a little differently. For example, a billboard may simply state: "Locally owned. Locally controlled." or "People, Not Profits" or "Where You Belong." Adapt the message to the communications channel you are using. And be clear, consistent, and creative.

Be clear. Remember that while you may know your operation inside and out, few outside the credit union's official family will know who you are, what you do, what you don't do, what you stand for, who your members are, what benefits you provide, or whether it's something they should care about.

Be consistent. Your communications need to withstand the test of time to be successful, which means you must formulate your communications for the long haul. They should carry the same theme and reinforce the same goals. "Just Do It" has been used to sell millions of pairs of running shoes, golf shoes, active wear, and other sports paraphernalia for years. And don't those three words—Just Do It—automatically produce the Nike company's trademark "swoosh" in your mind?

Be creative. Never before have so many people had so many ways to communicate. Ironically, the information age has actually increased the odds *against* getting your message across and having it acted upon. Only the most creative efforts have a fighting chance to cut through the clutter.

Reaching Your Audiences

What media should you use? The answer depends on whom you want to reach. You'll need to ask each media outlet for its media or advertiser kit. Here you'll find a wealth of information about who listens, reads, or watches. Match your audience with the media outlet to ensure that you are spending on placements that have the most impact and the most effect.

Ask each media outlet for its media or advertiser kit.

Your goal is to get the right message to the right audience at the right time. Carefully examine what group or groups you wish to reach. Although you may want everyone in your community to be aware of the credit union, it's tough to craft a message that strikes a responsive chord in the "general public," and it's even tougher to buy enough time and space to ensure that the message is heard and seen by them. Better to delineate more clearly exactly who it is you wish to reach: youth, seniors, first-time home buyers, business leaders, community groups, and so on. Then refine your message and use the media mix that is most likely to reach them. The media mix can include mass media outlets, such as radio, television, or newspaper ads, as well as newsletters; collateral materials, such as brochures and lobby displays; or special events or programs.

Special Programs

Novi Community Credit Union ($38 million in assets) in Novi, Michigan, seeks to demonstrate its commitment to the community by promoting financial literacy.

A primary example is a partnership with local schools. Susan Cusick, vice president, community development, not only makes classroom presentations at the middle and high school levels, but also works closely with elementary school teachers in developing curricula that teach economic and financial literacy concepts. These materials are designed to meet the standards and guidelines that are tested as part of Michigan's statewide assessment program. They are therefore well received by the teachers, who may have little experience or expertise in personal finance but are now expected to teach it. Cusick also brings students into the credit union on field trips and has worked with classes on semester-long projects. A marketing class, for example, developed a radio ad campaign for the credit union.

"Our goal is to get students to understand what a credit union is, the range of services offered, and what role they can have in it," Cusick says. "We take our commitment to the community very seriously," she adds. "We want to show that we're here as a neighbor that will not only write the check for a donation but also pitch in shoulder to shoulder."

John Deere Community Credit Union in Waterloo, Iowa, has special programs for every segment of its membership—from a Kirby Kangaroo Club for those twelve and younger to a Golden Passports program for members fifty and better. The senior club has some 2,100 members who receive special benefits including free services such as travelers' checks, share drafts, and money orders. They also have a newsletter and can participate in excursions to area attractions, bus trips to neighboring states, and educational seminars.

Programs geared to specific niches within the community and your membership are an excellent way to enhance the credit union's image. They bring focus to your activities and send a crystal clear message about what's important to your credit union.

PROTECTING YOUR IMAGE

The visibility that community credit unions enjoy presents both challenge and opportunity. The challenge lies in creating and protecting a positive image in the community. A positive image provides a firm foundation for growth. A negative image, on the other hand, can destroy a credit union's credibility—resulting in the loss of its members' trust and, eventually, that of the entire community.

EFFECTIVE COMMUNITY RELATIONS

Learner Objectives

Upon completion of this chapter, you will be able to

1. explain why "doing good" is good business;

2. initiate a strategic approach to community relations;

3. establish a community relations or social responsibility policy; and

4. identify the key elements of gaining positive publicity.

Taking an active role in improving the quality of life in the community is a strong credit union tradition. In fact, the International Credit Union Operating Principles specifically spell out "social goals" as a tenet of credit union philosophy: "Continuing the ideals and beliefs of cooperative pioneers, credit unions seek to bring about human and social development. Their vision of social justice extends both to the individual members and to the broader community within which the credit union and its members reside."

But for community credit unions, being a solid corporate citizen is not only the right thing to do, it's an essential business strategy. Putting the credit union philosophy of mutual self-help and "people helping people" into action not only achieves the greater good of "human and social development," it has important and beneficial side effects: greater visibility and an enhanced reputation. This, in turn, often translates to more business from current members and to attracting new members. There's no question that "doing good" is good business.

TAKE A STRATEGIC APPROACH

But, as with any business strategy, the effectiveness of your community relations program is contingent on how well your plans are conceived and carried out. Community activities are not free. Staff time is required. Monetary and "in-kind" contributions are necessary. There are opportunity costs to pay: What would you be engaged in if you were not involved with the community? You need a strategic approach to community involvement.

You need a strategic approach to community involvement.

That's not to say you won't accomplish anything if you take on projects haphazardly. It's not necessarily wrong to jump on the latest fund-raising bandwagon for someone who is seriously ill, or to have an emergency food drive when the food pantries are bare. You will, no doubt, be performing a public service. A well-planned and well-executed program, however, will maximize your effectiveness and make the best use of your time and effort.

You still can take on projects on an "as-needed" or emergency basis, but only as they fit within your overall strategic plan. For example, if one of your members needs a heart transplant, which is not covered by medical insurance, you have several options. If your overall plan includes criteria that put helping members in need as one of your objectives, then you would consider launching a full-fledged fund-raising campaign to collect the funds the member needs to have the operation. If your plan allows employees to perform public service or volunteer activities on credit union time, and the staff wants to help by placing collection canisters at teller stations and the reception desk, this might be your contribution. But if this cause, while legitimate, does not meet all of your criteria, you may wish to participate in it only minimally. Set up an account to receive donations and perhaps put up a poster in your lobby or contribute a small amount of money.

The point is that you should make a conscious decision about what causes you support so that you are not swept up in response to an emotional appeal or are not tempted to jump on a bandwagon because of outside pressure. The unhappy reality is that there are unlimited requests for your limited resources. You need to mindfully, not emotionally, allocate your time, effort, and money to the causes that will best serve your overall mission.

The unhappy reality is that there are unlimited requests for your limited resources.

Unfortunately, many organizations have community relations programs in place that are either a mishmash of pet projects of former and current executives and board members or an inflexible policy of giving to only certain agencies. While it's possible that these programs are effective, it's just as possible that there are other, more effective programs to implement.

If this describes the current status at your credit union, take heart. You won't be able to fix it overnight, but by investing some time in revamping the program, you'll put in place a program that best serves the community and your credit union.

NEEDS SURVEY

Start by researching community needs. This can either be assigned to staff or to a volunteer committee. Scan your local newspapers for articles on community problems and what is being done to address them. Check with United Way, community foundations, or local colleges to determine if any research studies have been conducted. As you review the existing data, think about how the issues that have been identified relate to your credit union's mission. For example, if the lack of affordable housing is a recurring theme, consider ways your credit union could help: partnering with groups such as Habitat for Humanity, donating to foundations that assist with down payments, or offering seminars to help people prepare for homeownership. At this point, however, you are simply in the brainstorming stage. Deciding what programs to implement should come later. As the existing research is reviewed, keep notes of your ideas about how the credit union can help solve some of the problems.

Gather Data

You may find little has been done to identify community needs, or that what you've gathered is dated due to changes in the environment. If so, you should conduct your own survey. You may want to do so even if the available data seem adequate. Your survey need not be elaborate. Begin by compiling a contact list. The list might include the following:

- United Way
- Community foundations
- Government offices (state, city, county, township, or village)
- Media
- Service organizations, chamber of commerce, community groups
- Schools
- Community leaders

Get names, addresses, and telephone numbers. Then write a letter explaining that you are seeking their perspective on community issues. Contact at least three or more organizations because each will have a different take on what issues the community is facing. This is to be expected. What you are looking for are recurring themes. For example, school administrators may identify gang activities as an issue. A community leader may cite lack of skilled labor. This may point to working on youth development activities.

Seek perspectives on community issues.

You can either include a short survey in the letter or follow up with a phone call and complete the inquiry over the phone. Ask your contacts for their views on the most compelling problems or issues facing the community and any further information or data they may have. Also ask for information on groups or initiatives that are seeking to address these problems. Get a brief description of the work being done and any contact information.

Survey as many groups as time and workload permit. You'll want to get as many perspectives as you can. Consider this: Your impression of a city viewed from an airplane traveling at 35,000 feet will vary from the one you get when you are walking down its main street.

Analyze the Data

Once you've gathered the data, it's time to analyze it in the context of your credit union's mission, goals, and objectives. This step is best taken by a group, ideally, a committee made up of staff and volunteers. The group should take a look at the findings of research done by other organizations and the survey done by the credit union. Consider the following:

- Do any patterns emerge?
- Are there recurring themes?
- What's being done currently to address these problems? Are these initiatives having any effect?

Next, discuss the credit union's mission. What goals and objectives have been set for the year? Now match up the information from your needs surveys and begin to identify projects that

- match the goals of your credit union;
- help solve the more compelling problems; and
- have the greatest chance of success.

Use your brainstorming ideas from your initial survey, but don't limit yourself. These should be your idea-starters and serve as jumping-off points for further discussion.

Plan Your Response

Here's an example of how the process might work. Your research identifies youth-related issues as one of the major concerns in the community. Your credit union's goals and objectives include increasing membership by 5 percent and increasing your business loans by 10 percent. This suggests that your community relations program should focus on outreach activities that touch youth and their parents and increase your visibility within the business community. Look for partners that can help you accomplish this. Do the high schools need sponsors for their marketing or DECA (distributive education) clubs? Is there a service club project that focuses on youth and families that needs volunteers? The key is to do your homework to find out what areas need attention and then get involved strategically.

THE ART OF STRATEGIC RELATIONSHIPS

By establishing relationships with the appropriate people and institutions you can leverage your community involvement activities, that is, you can increase the impact and effectiveness of your program by making strategic choices. Consider the questions listed in figure 5.1.

ESTABLISH A SOCIAL RESPONSIBILITY POLICY

Central to your community relations program is a social responsibility policy approved by the credit union's board of directors. The policy provides a platform

Figure 5.1 Questions to Answer in Building Strategic Community Relationships

- Are there specific groups you want to reach? For example, small-business owners, first-time home buyers, young professionals, immigrant groups?

- What community needs have you identified? How do these needs relate to your mission, your goals, and the groups you have identified as prospective members?

- Are there key people involved with the initiatives that you've identified? Can they open doors to new members or new marketing opportunities?

- What resources are you willing to donate? How much money? How much time? How many volunteers can you recruit from the board of directors, management and staff, and/or membership?

- What organizations are your employees and/or board members already involved in? Is it appropriate to build on those relationships? CUNA Mutual Group, for example, encourages and recognizes employee volunteerism with a program called "Dollars For Doers." The program recognizes outstanding employee volunteers by providing financial support to the nonprofit group at which they spend a significant part of their own time. Individuals donating at least fifty hours each year earn up to $500 for their nonprofit. Teams of employees also may participate and earn up to $1,000 for their charities.

from which to direct your community involvement and charitable activities. As difficult as it is to raise funds, it's just as hard to give money and other resources away. The policy can provide overall direction for your efforts, and will enable you to manage your corporate contributions and community relations efforts more effectively.

Policy Criteria

The policy should specify who will approve charitable contributions and/or donations. Some credit union boards retain this responsibility, and others delegate it to management. Whoever is responsible, funds should be disbursed based on a determination that the donations are in the best interests of the credit union and are reasonable, given the credit union's size and financial condition.

The policy should identify who is authorized to act and the extent of their authority. For example, the marketing director may be charged with reviewing and screening contribution requests and making recommendations for funding as well as selecting the credit-union-sponsored volunteer activities. The head teller may be authorized to approve time off for volunteer work, based on workload. The president may provide the final approval for funds and may select the volunteer functions the credit union will sponsor.

The social responsibility policy should include a statement of its objective—for example, to promote the credit union philosophy of mutual self-help and "people helping people" or "to improve the quality of life within the community using the cooperative principles."

The policy should specify the criteria the credit union will use to evaluate requests for funds or for volunteers. For example:

- How do the goals of the organization requesting help align overall with the credit union philosophy of cooperative self-help or specifically with the goals and objectives of the credit union?
- What is the current involvement of employees or credit union board/committee members?
- What past support did the credit union provide that produced positive results?
- What other organizations, if any, are providing support?

Decision-Making

Allocation of funds should also be specified. Use a percentage range—for example, 25 percent to 40 percent of contributions—so that there is some built-in flexibility. A rigid schedule may preclude you from taking advantage of an exceptional opportunity. Identify general categories, not specific agencies. Again, you need a flexible, but firm policy. Categories might include one or more of the following:

- Health and human services
- Education, training, and employment
- Children, youth, and families
- Community service and economic development
- Culture and the arts
- Conservation and the environment
- Tax-exempt organizations whose purpose is to promote and develop credit unions.

The policy also should state whether employees are allowed to volunteer on work time for organizations that meet your criteria, how many hours per year, and who can authorize time off. It also should indicate under what circumstances requests for in-kind products or services will be approved. For example, donating premium items or a no-cost share draft account.

Specifying which activities the credit union will *not* fund is also important. This can save everyone a lot of time. Federal credit unions, for example, cannot make donations to for-profit enterprises, or to groups located outside or that do not conduct business in the areas where the credit union is located.

The policy also should require that all requests be in writing. Some organizations, including credit unions, create a contributions request form to expedite the approval process.

DOING GOOD AND GETTING CREDIT

Supporting the community is a noble goal, but shouldn't be your only one. As a steward of your members' money, you have a responsibility to ensure that there is a return on the investment you make in charitable donations—whether in cash or staff support.

Following the steps outlined previously can help you make the most of "doing good." If you've matched community needs with your credit union's goals, you should see a payback eventually. For example, if you support a fund-raiser for a local Board of Realtors® that benefits a community housing foundation, chances are you will be able to nurture your relationship with the real estate community, a key element in a successful mortgage program. If you're involved in a service club program in which you meet and work with the owners of small businesses, you'll likely have a chance to introduce them to your business loan programs. If you provide credit union coloring books to a daycare center, you'll introduce the credit union to young families.

It's not enough to "do good." You also need to get credit for it.

But to ensure the best return on your investment, it's not enough to "do good." You also need to get credit for it. There are a variety of ways to accomplish this.

Don't just assume you will be recognized. Before you commit to a donation, find out what recognition the organization is providing and how many other sponsors they are seeking. If you are making a substantial contribution, you don't want to drown in a sea of logos on the back of a t-shirt. On the other hand, if your logo appears on the t-shirt and in a program, and you are able to display a banner prominently, this may suit your needs.

At events, bring your own banner or signage. This puts your name out there in a way you can control. You won't have to worry about tiny type or misspellings. If it's an event with multiple sponsors for which you have supplied volunteers, make sure your banner is displayed during their shift. For instance, if your credit union is staffing a fund-raising telethon that's being televised, make sure it's your banner that's visible to the camera, not the sign for the bank employees that had the previous shift or the shift following your credit union's.

Find out what kind of publicity the organization is planning. If you are a major sponsor, make sure you are included in the press release. Will there be an ad published in the newspaper to thank sponsors?

Keep your members informed. Include information about your community activities in your newsletter, on bulletin boards in your lobby, in statement stuffers, or drive-up envelopes. If appropriate, ask for volunteers or for monetary donations. At Alternatives Federal Credit Union in Ithaca, New York, for example, members can participate in its "Round-off Deposits" program. Members can round down a deposit to the nearest dollar, and the credit union donates the difference to a participating agency in the community.

Show your colors. If you allow employees to volunteer on work time and the event or occasion is such that they can wear some type of credit union apparel— for example, a sport or t-shirt with your logo on it—require it.

Remember, recognition is the fuel that keeps volunteers going. Both the credit union and the agency or organization you're supporting should highlight volunteers' efforts and thank volunteers at every possible occasion. Possible methods include newsletter features, "volunteer of the month" programs, recognition at the event by posting names and affiliations, t-shirts or hats, handwritten thank you notes, and an annual recognition event, such as a picnic, breakfast, or luncheon.

At Central Virginia Federal Credit Union, recognition is taken one step further: employees are rewarded for their involvement. As part of a comprehensive incentive program, employees receive one hour of leave time for every hour they volunteer on an approved volunteer project outside of normal business hours. The list of appropriate projects is compiled by the credit union's activities committee, made up of leadership and staff. In addition, each year the credit union chooses a single project or group to support as a corporate project; employees earn two hours of leave time for every hour of involvement. Certain other conditions must be met:

- Employees must get written approval of the group/event and indicate the number of hours they propose to work.
- Employees must wear a credit union shirt while volunteering.
- The charity must provide written material (brochure, flyer, newspaper article, etc.) to the credit union.
- Employees need to furnish a picture of themselves participating in the event.

The documentation serves two important purposes. It provides an internal control regarding the volunteer activity, and it's compiled into notebooks that are not only shared with members, but also with legislators. Tracking hours provides valuable evidence of the credit union's service to the community and is a powerful lobbying tool.

Tracking hours provides valuable evidence of the credit union's service to the community and is a powerful lobbying tool.

Supporting community programs is no time for modesty. Make sure the credit union is recognized for its contributions, too. Don't be afraid to ask for it either. Sometimes, nonprofits become complacent and start taking their volunteers and supporters for granted. If you are unhappy with the way you are being treated, it may be appropriate to find new partners.

GET INVOLVED

Community relations is not a passive activity for any organization, and particularly not for community credit unions. An effective community relations program can greatly influence how members and potential members perceive the credit union. It can also send powerful messages to key audiences, including legislators, the media, and opinion leaders. Community relations should be viewed strategically, not as an afterthought or superfluous to the credit union's mission.

FROM OCCUPATIONAL TO COMMUNITY COMMON BONDS: MANAGING THE TRANSITION

Learner Objectives

Upon completion of this chapter, you will be able to

1. identify the trends relating to charter conversions;

2. recognize the additional challenges faced by community credit unions; and

3. identify the issues that must be addressed in managing the transition.

Organizing credit unions—a primary mission of the U.S. credit union movement in its adolescent years—has nearly become a lost art. Credit union pioneers like Roy Bergengren, Louise McCarren Herring, Dora Maxwell, and Tom Doig organized postal workers, church goers, union members, firefighters, grocery store employees—virtually any group they could find. Tom Doig, alone, organized more than a thousand credit unions in his career.

TODAY'S CHANGING SCENARIO

Times have changed. Now few people are inducted annually into CUNA's Founder's Club, the roll of credit union organizers. Most who are inducted have organized community development credit unions. That's because economic and social conditions have conspired to make organizing a credit union serving an occupational group or a mainstream community a rare achievement. Today's workers are more likely to work in a small business than a giant factory. Home offices abound. Banks, mutual funds, and other financial services organizations compete fiercely for the middle-class market. Previously, organizing a credit union involved a minimum of 200 people who shared a common bond. Now NCUA's IRPS-99 specifies a group of 3,000 as potentially viable for a stand-alone credit union.

While there are fewer credit unions, more people than ever enjoy the benefits of credit union membership.

The number of credit unions continues to shrink from a peak of some 23,876 credit unions in 1969 to fewer than half that number today. Most of the decline is the result of smaller credit unions facing economic pressure, or simply being unable to offer the services their members want and therefore merging into larger credit unions so members can have access to these services at a credit union. A group of 200 people seeking credit union services would face enormous difficulty in raising the human and monetary capital needed to start a credit union. Now they would gain access to a credit union as a "select employee group" (SEG) or "select group." So while there are fewer credit unions, more people than ever enjoy the benefits of credit union membership: more than 76 million, or more than triple the number in 1969.

PATHS TO SURVIVAL

Although some community development credit unions have straddled the regulatory and economic hurdles in gaining a charter, usually a community will gain a credit union due to a charter conversion. A typical scenario: An occupationally based credit union is merged with another credit union. Now the "new" credit union has additional space and resources and serves a wider range of membership. SEGs are added. Expanding the field of membership to include the entire community is a natural next step, particularly if the original field of membership is experiencing an employment decline.

Such was the case for Decibel Credit Union, a $45 million credit union in Pueblo, Colorado. Originally, the credit union served employees of U.S. West, AT&T, and Western Electric. Cataclysmic changes in the telecommunications industry had dramatic repercussions for Decibel. The credit union lost members. One company that employed 900 people closed, and another that employed 1,200 now has 225. Decibel added several select employee groups and merged with a smaller credit union, but it was not enough to stem the tide. The credit union sought and gained a community charter in order to survive. The charter expansion allows the credit union to serve Pueblo County, a potential field of membership of 136,000 residents. Notes the credit union's president, John Carpio: "We had to go with a community charter to pick up our earnings and begin to lend to the younger generation."

Because its membership is largely made up of retirees, the credit union plans to attract younger people—high school and college students and those just entering the workforce—through extensive use of technology, including a bill payer option on its web site. The web site also allows residents of rural Pueblo County to access the credit union more easily.

Heartland Credit Union, a $70 million community credit union in Madison, Wisconsin, took a similar path to a community charter. Although Heartland was originally chartered to serve employees of Wisconsin Bell, divestiture, downsizing, and relocation began to take their toll. "The handwriting was on the wall," notes Joyce Harris, president. Mergers—first with a hospital employees credit union and then with other small credit unions—expanded the field of membership. Now the credit union's charter allows it to serve people living and working in five Wisconsin counties.

Previously, the $40 million Central Virginia Federal Credit Union served a single sponsor, a naval defense contractor. When a big government contract was cancelled in 1991, employment plummeted. Recognizing its vulnerability and not wanting to be at the mercy of a single sponsor, the credit union changed its name, added groups, and began to plan for a community charter, which was granted in 1998. The credit union now serves residents of four counties. Credit unions converting to community charters often experience great opportunities for growth. They also face challenges, some of which are listed in figure 6.1.

Figure 6.1 Community Credit Union Challenges

Whether by birth or rebirth, credit unions with community charters face these challenges:

- Higher operating expense-to-gross income ratios due to higher delivery costs.
- More branches resulting in higher fixed assets costs.
- Bigger marketing and education budgets.
- More complex risk management.

GOVERNANCE ISSUES

Expanding a credit union's field of membership also may require efforts to expand representation on the board of directors and supervisory, credit, and other committees. While there's no requirement to seek geographic representation, it's difficult for a board or committee made up solely of individuals from the original sponsor to bring all perspectives to the table. In addition, policy decisions become more complex when they affect a broad range of people. Board members with a variety of backgrounds, experiences, and expertise are better able to define the problems and come up with alternative solutions.

Recruit Board Members

Board members may have to be recruited. In a world where time-saving devices have the opposite effect—merely allowing people to take on increasing numbers of commitments—that may not be an easy task. Just as recruiting employees in a tight labor market requires creativity, so does finding candidates for board and committee positions.

Just as recruiting employees in a tight labor market requires creativity, so does finding candidates for board and committee positions.

A nominating committee or board development committee should be charged with the responsibility. One helpful tool is to create a grid specifying what skills and expertise are currently represented on the board. This might include planning, financial, legal, personnel, marketing, or product/service expertise. The grid helps identify what is lacking. The committee also should devise a simple application form that asks for biographical information, skills, and capabilities the potential applicant hopes to bring to the board and expects to take away, and any questions he or she might have.

The committee also should develop a list of potential candidates. You could, for example, invite about twenty community leaders—the type of people you'd like to have serve on the board, but suspect would not be interested in doing so because of other commitments—to a breakfast or lunch. Tell them that this is a one-meeting committee in which you'll provide information about the credit union and what you're looking for in a board member. At the conclusion of the meeting, they'll be asked to provide the name of one person they think would be a good board member. Following the meeting, members of the nominating committee should call these referrals, indicate who recommended them, and then invite them to be candidates.

Prospects should then meet with the president and the board chair to learn more about the credit union, find out if there are any conflicts of interest, and determine whether they should be encouraged to run for election. If your bylaws require it, collect a minimum number of member signatures to place the name on the ballot.

Recruiting board members may represent a dramatic change for your credit union, and therefore, as with any change, be threatening to some individuals. Expect that some will be unhappy with the prospect. Strong leadership from the board may be needed to facilitate the process.

Orient New Members

Once new board members are elected, an orientation session will help ensure that both old and new members are prepared to fulfill their roles and responsibilities. Typically, the board chair and the credit union president facilitate the session, although the services of an outside facilitator may be appropriate in some cases. The orientation should cover these topics:

- Introduction and brief background on all board members
- The credit union's mission, vision, and values statement
- A brief history of the credit union

- The policy manual
- Roles and responsibilities of the board and the staff
- Organizational chart, including short biographies of key staff
- Calendar of events, including board meetings, committee meetings, special events at the credit union, educational conferences, and other important dates
- Sample agendas and information about how the board conducts its meetings

Plan plenty of time for questions and answers as well as time before and after the meeting for social interaction. If appropriate, a current member of the board should be assigned as a mentor or partner to help orient a new board member, which can be done formally or informally.

Assess Board Performance

The board of directors also should conduct a self-evaluation routinely to assess how well the board is fulfilling its responsibilities. This will help identify the areas in which the board members feel they are doing a good job as well as those where improvement is needed. The self-evaluation need not be complex; it is simply a tool to help focus attention on the strengths and weaknesses of the board. Figure 6.2 provides a sample self-evaluation form.

Each board member should evaluate the board's performance candidly. The statements receiving the lowest total scores are the areas where the board feels it's doing a good job. Conversely, the highest scores are the areas in which the board should focus its attention on improvements.

OPERATIONAL CHANGES

The transition to a community credit union also may require some management reorganization and operational changes. You had to run the numbers in preparing your business plan to make the case for your conversion. But putting the plan into action requires the cooperation of many people, not all of whom are interested in cooperating. Some may even have an interest in creating conflict! This can create turmoil. For example, the decision to close an on-site branch and replace it with an ATM may not be greeted enthusiastically by the members who use that branch regularly. Keep in mind that while members may understand intellectually why

Figure 6.2 Assessing Board Performance

Rate the following statements on a scale of 1 to 5: "1" indicates that you "strongly agree" with the statement and "5" indicates that you "strongly disagree."

_____ Board members and staff are aware of and understand their respective roles.

_____ The board provides clearly written qualifications and expectations for the credit union's president.

_____ Board members understand the credit union's mission.

_____ Board members understand the credit union's products and services.

_____ Board members make policy-related decisions.

_____ Staff provide regular reports to the board on key areas.

_____ Board members represent the membership effectively.

_____ All necessary skills and backgrounds are represented on the board.

_____ Each board member has a policy manual and has read it.

_____ Board members participate actively in the planning process and follow up regularly on goals and action plans.

_____ Board meetings run efficiently, focus on important credit union matters, and all board members participate.

_____ The board has a process for reviewing and updating policies.

_____ A plan is in place to ensure director training and education.

Add total points and divide by 13 for the overall score. A score of 1–2 indicates the board is doing a good job of fulfilling its obligations.

you need to do so, they may have an emotional attachment to the branch and may be angry that you are taking it away from them. They're likely to take it out on your frontline employees. It's critical that you keep them informed about decisions and the rationale behind them. Remember, nature abhors a vacuum. If you don't provide forthright information, rumors and misinformation will work their way down a grapevine faster than any other communication media. Use the tips in figure 6.3 to keep employees informed of credit union plans.

Figure 6.3 Keep Employees Informed

Your employees need to know about changes that will occur as a result of the conversion to a community charter. Ideally, the information should be presented face-to-face in a staff meeting, including a handout. A "frequently asked questions" format is an efficient way to communicate. Questions to address should include:

- When will the conversion take place?

- Will there be any event?

- Will any employees lose their jobs or have major changes in responsibilities?

- Why are we converting to a community charter?

- Will any branches close? Will we have new branches?

- Will our name change?

- Will we add any services?

- Will our hours change?

- Will there be anything in the news about it?

- What are we supposed to tell members?

Be sure your employees are informed before any information is released to members, the media, or the general public. Without advance information, your employees may be in the position of having members wave letters or newsletters in their faces without having any clue about what was announced.

THE NAME GAME

The transition from occupational to community charter may not be complete without a name change to reflect your broader scope. Many credit unions simply add the word "community" to their name to signal that membership is now open to more than the employees and family members of the original sponsor. This is a way to stay connected to the original sponsor in a tangible way. Credit unions that have undergone a conversion emphasize that it's important not to forget "your roots." Long-time loyal members should not feel as though you are abandoning them in your efforts to grow. Communicate how expanding the membership will benefit both the credit union as an institution and the credit union's members individually.

This should be your primary theme in preparing your current members for the change and in making the announcement. Send this message in more than one way. A small article in your newsletter will not adequately set the stage for a smooth transition. Your member communication plan should include such items as:

- Fact sheet
- Frequently Asked Questions (FAQs) sheet
- Newsletter article
- Letter to members from board chair and president
- Informal and formal membership meetings
- Telephone hotline
- Telephone message-on-hold system
- Web site information and e-mail for questions
- Lobby counter cards and posters
- Open house

Get current members involved in the process. This might include a "member get a member" promotional campaign that rewards current members for recruiting new members. This can take the form of cash or merchandise and/or contest or sweepstakes. As there are specific legal considerations regarding contests, check with your legal counsel before launching this type of promotion.

Create a timeline for introducing new materials. Use the corporate identity checklist in chapter 4 as a guide to determine what needs to be changed. Allow members to continue to use share drafts and plastic cards with the previous name. To speed the transition, provide an incentive for members to turn in their share drafts with your old name. For example, provide a free box of share drafts for every box turned in.

Only after you have communicated with your internal audiences adequately—your employees and your members—should your public campaign be launched. Advertising and public relations efforts can include media such as newspaper, magazine, radio, and television ads; billboards; press releases; feature stories; announcements on your web site and web advertising; and an open house "grand opening" celebration.

Complete name changes—from Widget Employees Credit Union to What-a-Deal Credit Union—require the help of experts. Hire a communications firm that specializes in name and logo development. The firm should work with you to come up with a new name and logo that matches your identity. The firm should include a trademark attorney on the team or request that you hire one. Potential new names need to be researched and the one you choose needs to be registered as a trade name. Don't forget to reserve your Internet-domain name, and trademark it as well.

RISK MANAGEMENT

According to the Nonprofit Risk Management Center, a service group located in Washington, D.C., risk management recognizes and responds to dangers that interfere with services and operations. To be effective, a risk management program must

- identify threats by acknowledging and specifying risks;
- control loss—by preventing loss and reducing the severity should a loss occur;
- implement safeguards against unauthorized use of funds;
- protect against injury;
- take appropriate action to ensure legal compliance;
- select adequate risk management tools, including insurance; and
- evaluate results and revise strategies accordingly.

Keep in mind that risk management is more than just insurance; think of insurance as a safety net and only one tool of many in an effective risk management program.

Identifying Risks

Although no credit union is exempt from implementing the proper internal controls and security measures to manage its risk, community credit unions tend to face more complex risk management issues. Their increased visibility and exposure attracts more than just potential members. To the armed robber, burglar, forger, or bad check artist, a community credit union is an appealing opportunity.

According to CUMIS RISK Management, most losses occur because

- personnel ineffectively implement standard operating procedures;
- employees lack up-to-date written operating policies, procedures, and guidelines to follow; and
- employees are unaware of crime trends and the techniques used by con artists and other criminals.

Studies indicate that financial institutions, including credit unions, typically have a master manual of operational policies and procedures, but the copies distributed at the department level often are not updated. Furthermore, managers and supervisors often fail to read the manual, and the procedures are not supervised or enforced. This creates the opportunity, environment, and circumstances for a loss.

In addition, on-the-job training for new employees is often the "show-and-tell" method. The new employee shadows the longer-term employee, learning about the processes and procedures through observation and verbal instruction. This can serve to institutionalize improper procedures, however, because the experienced employee may not be precisely accurate in performing the functions. This results in the bad habits of one employee being passed on to the next.

Protecting Against Loss

Follow specific, written guidelines when training employees. The guidelines should include a complete, up-to-date procedures manual, checklists that summarize the credit union's standard operating procedures, and an explanation of why each step in the process is important and necessary. Be sure the guidelines are easy to understand and to follow. A common error in procedures manuals is overestimating the employee's knowledge. Make sure the directions are clear by asking someone—preferably someone unfamiliar with the material—to perform a task using the directions as a guide. The feedback from this exercise will assist you in clearly delineating the process.

A common error in procedures manuals is overestimating the employee's knowledge.

CUNA Mutual's Scam Alert is a proactive attempt to reduce forgery losses. Scam Alert receives information on fraudulent activity from credit unions and law enforcement agencies and then uses it to detect trends, track activity, and identify the people involved. By communicating the "who," "what," "where," and "how" of the scam and recommending immediate action, Scam Alert provides a way for credit unions to recognize and foil further forgery attempts. To report a scam or receive information about the program, call (800) 356-2644, ext. 7192, or visit the members' section of CUNA Mutual's web site at *www.cunamutual.com*. Current scams also are reported regularly in *Credit Union Magazine's* "News Now" on CUNA's web site: *www.cuna.org*.

Protecting Your Employees

While con artists use their wits to defraud, armed robbers or burglars use more physical means. The chance of burglary—generally defined as a loss from unauthorized, forcible entry during nonbusiness hours—can be reduced through the use of reasonable security measures. These include site selection, appropriate exterior designs and building materials, steel gates, and so on. Because community credit unions tend to have branches, they are at increased exposure to burglary.

Unfortunately, the possibility of a robbery is always present. There are measures that can be taken to reduce the loss, but there are no guarantees even if they are taken. That said, your credit union must take steps to protect its employees and reduce their vulnerability. These include the following precautions:

1. Limit currency to only what is needed. Conduct a cash-flow analysis to find out your currency needs. This not only reduces the credit union's vulnerability to an armed robbery, it has the added bonus of keeping funds earning interest.

2. Control access to all cash items, including currency, travelers checks, and so on, by keeping them in individually lockable containers such as trays, drawers, safes, or vaults. Spread out large cash item exposures. Count currency in a controlled area that can't be observed.

3. Control unauthorized access in the teller area by using physical barriers.

4. Ensure alarm systems and surveillance cameras are working properly.

5. Consider bullet-resistive barriers. Properly installed, these provide the maximum access control.

6. Keep entrances, exits, and the lobby area free of obstacles that provide camouflage and concealment for a would-be robber.

7. Locate teller stations that handle large currency amounts at the greatest distance from the exit. This slows the robber's escape and gives the surveillance system an extra measure of time.

8. Caution staff not to be lured away by distractions—possibly staged by the criminals—thus leaving the station unprotected.

9. Request police protection when handling unusually large amounts of cash, and alert them to any suspicious persons or circumstances in the area.

10. Offer a standing invitation for neighborhood police to stop in for coffee anytime during office hours and to use your parking lot to write up their reports.

---

11. Conduct training sessions that emphasize what to expect and how to act during an armed robbery. Involve your local police force. Emphasize that once the robber enters the credit union, life safety should be everyone's sole concern. At no time should anyone attempt to stop the robber.

Making Your Move

Making the transition from occupational to community charter starts with the business plan submitted to your regulator. But that's only the beginning. From the makeup of the board of directors to revisions in your operations to a name change to managing increased risk, it will take considerable effort and planning on the part of all members of your team to put the plan into action and ensure a smooth transition to serving the entire community.

LOCATION, LOCATION, LOCATION

Learner Objectives

Upon completion of this chapter, you will be able to

1. explain the importance of location; and

2. weigh the advantages and disadvantages of using technology in place of brick-and-mortar.

In the real estate business, there's a saying that the most important factor affecting a buyer's decision is location. It's also the second most important, and the third. The same can be said for a consumer's choice in financial institution: location is everything. Consider these scenarios:

- A credit union serving military personnel finds itself "off limits" to the community if it expands its charter, but retains its only office on the base.

- Road construction slows lobby traffic to a trickle just as a mortgage loan promotion is launched.

- The empty lot the credit union leases for parking is sold to a developer.

- Migration to the suburbs chokes off retail business in the city's center; the credit union located there is now surrounded by empty buildings frequented only by vandals.

It's easy to see that each of these credit unions is "geographically challenged." Consumers have high expectations regarding convenience. In fact, traditionally, credit union members have cited convenience as their major reason for joining credit unions. CUNA's National Member Survey has found that because so many members belong to employer-sponsored credit unions, they can conveniently transact their financial business at their workplace.

Traditionally, credit union members have cited convenience as their major reason for joining credit unions.

But as credit unions move outside the workplace, they face many of the same challenges retailers of all types of products and services must deal with. If a location is inconvenient or is perceived to be inconvenient, consumers must be provided with an incentive that triumphs over that obstacle. For credit unions, this may mean emphasizing the other attractions frequently cited by members as the reasons they joined the credit union: dividends on savings, reasonable rates on loans, and payroll deduction. Or it may mean relocation or opening additional branches.

Branch location is a good way for a community credit union to manage the transition from an occupationally based credit union, because a branch can be a way to build member loyalty. Often, members perceive the branch as *the* credit union. Consider the factors listed in figure 7.1 when opening a branch facility.

HIGH TOUCH OR HIGH TECH?

Another critical issue is whether a physical branch is needed at all. In a white paper developed for the National Association of Community Credit Unions, titled *Brick and Mortar Versus Technology,* Peter Simonson and Gary Nater, RSM McGladrey, Inc., point out that branch transactions declined 2 percent in 1998, while telephone transactions increased 3 percent, and ATM use increased 4 percent. Yet, branches are used more regularly than any other delivery channel, with close to nine of ten U.S. households visiting a credit union branch at least once a month, according to Robert Morris and Associates.

Research by Mentis Research Corporation found that people who use self-service options consistently account for just 20 percent of income. The 40 percent of members who never use self-service options account for 60 percent of a traditional

Figure 7.1 Facility Checklist

Assess the following factors when considering a location for relocating a main office or opening a branch office.

- *Facilities.* Should you buy, build, or lease? What is the effect on your capital if you decide to buy or build? What are your options when the lease expires and the landlord triples the rent?

- *Street access.* How does traffic flow? Will most people need to make a left-hand turn? Are turns allowed? Is there parking available? Is the drive-up easy to use?

- *Hours.* What is the community standard? What are the competition's standards? Are supermarket branch banks open ten hours a day, seven days a week?

- *Security.* What risk management measures are needed? Video cameras? Adequate outdoor lighting? Do plantings or landscaping detract from security? Do you need a security guard, bullet-proof glass, double-entry way? What are the crime statistics for the area?

- *ADA compliance.* Are access requirements, mandated by the Americans with Disabilities Act, being met?

- *Population patterns.* Is the area growing? Are there development plans or zoning conflicts? What are the projected demographics of the area? High-density housing or estate homes?

- *Neighbors.* What other businesses share the immediate area? Will members be attracted or repelled by their proximity?

- *Profitability and productivity.* What are the projected operating costs? How many new and existing members do you expect to serve? What will it take in loan originations to pay for the office in a specified time frame, say five years?

credit union's income. In other words, some of credit unions' most profitable members tend to use branches consistently. Just as computer keyboards have not eliminated pens and paper, the availability of technology has not killed off the need for physical branches.

Rapid advances in technology have made "virtual branches" a reality. For many consumers, taking care of financial business is done at the click of a mouse, eliminating the need to drive to a facility, then find a place to park or get in line at the drive-up. They also aren't limited to conducting their business during business hours. Home financial services are transacted one of two ways: through a proprietary dial-up account or through the Internet. With a dial-up system, the member installs special software provided by the credit union, then dials a designated number via modem and uses the software to access accounts. An Internet-based system allows members to use a World Wide Web browser, such as Netscape Navigator or Internet Explorer, to reach the credit union's web site and access their accounts. Internet-based systems tend to be easier for members to use because once they've learned how to use their browser, contacting the credit union online requires only a password and a few additional steps.

But going online is not a panacea. According to Cyber Dialogue, a New York-based research firm, of the 9.4 million consumers who once completed their financial services transactions online, 3.1 million no longer do so. For example, between July 1998 and July 1999, some 2.2 million new customers signed on, but another 2.1 million consumers checked out. Reasons included:

- Too complicated or time consuming
- Unhappy with customer service
- No need or not interested
- Concerned about security or fraud
- Too costly
- Concerned about privacy

A study by Mentis Research Corporation found that only 4 percent of credit union members reported a desire for computer banking.

When automated teller machines were first introduced in the 1970s, some experts predicted that eventually they would eliminate the need for staffed branches. ATMs rack up $650 billion in transactions each year, according to *Bank Rate Monitor*. But the market is so saturated that the number of shipments worldwide rose only 4 percent in 1998 after a 25 percent growth rate in 1997. Some 140,000 ATMs were in use in the United States in 1997, up from the 75,000 in operation in 1990. But while ATMs are replacing tellers for routine transactions, particularly withdrawals, the number of financial institution branches has actually grown. Clearly, people want both the convenience of ATMs and the reassurance of conducting business face-to-face. According to a study conducted by KPMG Peat Marwick, two-thirds of customers prefer to avoid ATMs for some kinds of transactions, such as deposits.

In determining how to serve their members, credit unions must balance meeting member demand with cost considerations. There's no doubt that electronic delivery systems do save money. According to information from the CUNA 1997 Branch Operations Institute, while it costs $1.50 per transaction to deliver services at a branch, it's 76 cents via a telephone, 38 cents at an ATM, 2 cents with a dial-up account, and merely a penny via the Internet.

> *Finding the right combination of "high tech" and "high touch"*
> *is particularly critical for community credit unions, whose*
> *members may be spread over a wide geographic area.*

Finding the right combination of "high tech" and "high touch" is particularly critical for community credit unions, whose members may be spread over a wide geographic area.

SITE SELECTION

To serve its members in four counties, Lynchburg-based Central Virginia Federal Credit Union deployed ATMs in partnership with McDonald's restaurants. "The family image of McDonald's was a good fit for us," notes Bill Farley, president. The credit union also serves its members through an audio response system, a call center, participation in the Credit Union Shared Service Center shared branching network, and PC branching on its web site. The credit union also plans on adding a series of branches, for a total of six when expansion is completed.

In their white paper, Simonson and Nater suggest the following questions be addressed to aid in the branch and site selection process:

- What have you done in your current market area that has made you successful?
- Do you serve a particular niche in your current market(s)?
- What are the greatest challenges you have faced in your market area, for example, competition or market pressure?
- Have you done as well as you feel you could in your current market?
- What are your major growth and profitability goals for the next five years?
- Is the addition of a branch likely to contribute to the success of those goals?

- What similarities exist between your current and proposed market areas?

- What brought your attention to the area under study?

- What are the critical factors for success for a new location?

- What amount of resources will be dedicated to this location, including facility, personnel, and marketing resources?

- How will operations, such as staffing, data processing, and proof and data capture, be handled at this location?

- What data processing system are you currently using? Is it in-house or at a service center?

SHARED BRANCHING

Shared branching is a time-tested concept that puts the International Credit Union operating principle of "cooperation among cooperatives" into operation. Credit unions in Michigan, for example, have used a shared facility for more than twenty years. There are some 430 locations for credit unions in the Shared Service Center system. Members can search the center's web site at *www.creditunion.net* to find a location in their area. Services include deposits, withdrawals, loan payments, transfers, share draft cashing, money orders, travelers checks, statement printing, and telephone access to the member's credit union. Future services include automated lending, bill payment, kiosks, and an ATM network.

Increasingly, kiosks are playing a role in providing convenient electronic transactions. One study estimated a 35 percent compound annual growth rate for seven years straight. A kiosk usually has a computer with a hard disk and a CD-ROM drive, a monitor, and audiovisual capacity. Members use a keyboard, mouse, keypad, touch screen, microphone, and/or video camera. Heartland Credit Union in Madison, Wisconsin, for example, uses a kiosk to serve its rural members around the clock. Its bill-payer function and information about commodity markets are two popular features.

ALTERNATIVE BRANCHES

In-store branches are popping up in supermarkets, convenience stores, and discount stores across the country. In Dubuque, Iowa, DuTrac Community Credit Union opened a branch in a Wal-Mart following two years of discussions.

According to *Credit Union Newswatch,* once initial concerns about the credit union's inability to serve the general public were resolved, Wal-Mart didn't require much of DuTrac. The company only asked that DuTrac open a full-service branch and be open fifty hours a week, including eight hours on Saturday, "which was fine with us," according to DuTrac CEO Tom Sarvis. DuTrac's branch at Wal-Mart is a full-service branch with several tellers, a member service representative, and a branch manager, who can offer all types of loans. The credit union cannot serve nonmembers, for example, by cashing checks for them, but it can offer membership to people who live or work in the community. The branch provides an ATM that is open to the public.

A benefit of in-store branches is that the breakeven point is usually eighteen months, compared with the thirty-six months required for traditional brick-and-mortar branches.

In-store branches can range from full-service operations like DuTrac's, to fully automated systems with ATMs and video monitors. One trend is a modular design that can be easily assembled, typically in less than three days. If the credit union finds the branch is not economically feasible, it can just as easily be disassembled and transferred elsewhere. A benefit of in-store branches is that the breakeven point is usually eighteen months, compared with the thirty-six months required for traditional brick-and-mortar branches.

Minibranches can be found in strip malls, shopping centers, or as stand-alone branches. These smaller branches require decreased staffing levels. Typically, their customer base is less stable than an in-store branch. A supermarket, for example, usually has regular customers thereby increasing the probability that the in-store branch will as well. But a minibranch in a parking lot does not have this advantage. A minibranch in a strip mall does provide an opportunity to test market a branch location. Leases are generally short, so there's no long-term commitment to the location. Another possibility is to open a minibranch in one location specializing in mortgages or another elsewhere that only takes auto loan applications.

A *drive-up branch* is another low-cost option. It is typically smaller with low overhead and located near a brick-and-mortar branch. Often, drive-up branches are used to divert transaction traffic from the lobby of the nearby branch.

And while no one has introduced a telephone that can dispense cash, for many members the credit union is only a few touchtones away. *Interactive voice response or audio response systems* are not new. They've been around for nearly twenty years and originally were used primarily for checking balances and the status of share drafts. However, capabilities have improved and more services are available. Now, twenty-four hours a day, seven days a week, members can make loan or credit card payments, transfer balances, order checks, order copies of cancelled checks, or stop payments. They can even activate their credit cards.

Note, however, that members may need assistance in learning how to use audio response. The *Credit Union Executive's* 1998 Remote Access and Technology Survey Report found that 84 percent of credit unions offering audio response reported that it was one of the services with which members needed the most help.

CALL CENTERS

Call centers are another way to establish a "24/7" presence without building an additional branch. Call centers provide personal service because members communicate with people rather than a computer-generated voice. However, many credit unions outsource the function to avoid hiring additional staff. This raises some concerns about the ability of operators to handle inquiries; they may not be knowledgeable enough about your services. Take steps to ensure that quality control measures are in place.

Many credit unions outsource the call center function to avoid hiring additional staff.

Call centers can take routine calls about balance inquiries and rate and service questions. They can also speed up the process of applying for a consumer or mortgage loan. Call centers can take a loan application in eight to twelve minutes, and using predefined parameters, score the loan in seven to ten seconds. If the loan is marginal, a credit officer reviews it, and can provide conditional approval in three to five minutes more. While the approval may come with a long list of conditions, consumers are then directed to the credit union to complete the transaction.

IDENTIFYING COMFORT ZONES

Movie buffs may remember the scene in *Back to the Future* in which Michael J. Fox's character is astounded when he encounters gas station attendants who fill the gas tank, check the oil, and even clean the windshield. While consumers in some states still experience this personal service, many more are accustomed to "self-serve." As technology advances, more and more members may become accustomed to the "self-serve" financial products the credit union offers. However, members are at different places along the technology continuum. Few members will want to use technology for every transaction. What's convenient and comfortable *for them* at any given time will be the primary determinant.

THE PRODUCT MIX

Finding the right product mix to serve members' financial needs is a challenge for all credit unions. But for community credit unions that must go toe-to-toe with banks, it's essential. Because of the increased operational expenses involved with serving the entire community, a community credit union must work especially hard to capture all of its members' financial services business. Becoming a member's primary financial institution (PFI) is a "win-win" situation: Members use the credit union for all it's worth, paying less and getting more. The credit union gains economies of scale and increased efficiencies, thereby improving its profitability. Those profits, in turn, can be shared with members in the form of better rates and improved services.

Mortgages Are Key

Just as charity begins at home, so does the member's choice of a primary financial institution. A home loan is the shortest route to becoming a member's PFI. Research studies show repeatedly that the mortgage transaction creates the strongest bond between the member and the credit union. Members with mortgages typically use twice the number of products and services from their credit union. Mortgages also can provide fee and investment income as well as decrease the credit union's dependence on consumer and auto lending.

Members with mortgages typically use twice the number of products and services from their credit union.

While many credit unions, particularly community credit unions, have offered mortgages for many years, credit unions, in general, have not been major players in the mortgage arena. Federal credit unions are relative newcomers to the mortgage lending business, having only gained the authority to offer mortgages in 1978. During the 1990s, the credit union market share averaged 1.77 percent of the U.S. mortgage origination market. At mid-year 1999, credit unions had gained ground, with a 2.2 percent market share.

Less than 7 percent of U.S. credit union members chose their credit union for their mortgage needs, which means that 93 percent are going elsewhere for mortgage loans. This contributes to a "Catch 22": Because members don't use the credit union as their primary source of mortgage loans, they don't perceive the credit union as being the place to go for a home loan. They don't view the credit union as a place to get a mortgage because they have never used it for that purpose. Breaking that cycle requires a marketing plan that establishes your identity as a mortgage lender and sets you apart from the competition. In fact, don't assume members even know that you offer mortgage loans. That means you must market mortgage loans consistently, for example, not just in the spring when people are buying or building homes or when interest rates are low.

Real Estate Agents: Challenge and Opportunity

An additional challenge to capturing member's mortgage business is the critical role real estate agents play in the purchase of a home. Real estate agents can have a strong influence on where home buyers go for a mortgage—particularly first-time home buyers who are unfamiliar with the process and rely on their agent for advice. Because they get paid on commission, real estate agents are anxious to close the deal and close it quickly. That often means recommending a bank they've worked with in the past.

In some cases, real estate agents view credit unions as inept with regard to mortgage loans. They perceive credit unions as a place for car loans or personal loans, not mortgage loans. Or they have no reason to even think about whether the buyer belongs to a credit union. Here's where community credit unions enjoy a natural advantage over credit unions without an expanded field of membership. Building a relationship with real estate agents is easier if the agents know that virtually any of their clients are members or potential members of the credit union. It is also expedient and effective to use a greater variety of marketing tools, as described in figure 8.1.

Product and Market Positioning

Differentiating your products and services from the competition's allows your credit union to establish a strong product position. This may be accomplished in a number of ways including by price, service quality, ease of use, speed of service, or other special features.

According to CUNA's 1999 Environmental Scan, the new service standard is "24/7": twenty-four hours a day, seven days a week. "Nowhere is this standard more evident than in the changing world of mortgage lending," the Scan reports. E-commerce is revolutionizing the entire process. As many as ten basis points can be shaved off the loan's interest-rate cost because of the efficiencies of online applications, interest-rate locks, twenty-minute approval times, and the ability to originate and close a mortgage within thirty days—the new standard framework.

The mortgage lending business has always been extremely competitive and today's technology has pumped up the volume even more. To keep pace, credit

Figure 8.1 Marketing Tools

Community credit unions can use a wider variety of media more effectively than can closed-bond credit unions. All credit unions can use any of these promotional tools.

- Direct mail
- Brochures
- Statement stuffers
- Newsletters
- Posters

- Lobby displays
- Education seminars
- Web site
- Audio response system
- Advertising specialties

But community credit unions have the following additional tools, and they don't have to deal with "wasted" circulation.

- News releases
- Community home-buying fairs
- Yellow Pages advertisements
- Newspaper ads
- Radio

- Television and cable
- Signs and billboards
- Community events
- Sponsorship of parades, sporting events, and other events

unions must evaluate their mortgage programs constantly. This evaluation includes, but is not limited to, shopping the competition, conducting member surveys, updating technology, and performing quality control checks.

To establish a strong market position, a credit union must gain credibility.

Educating Members

To establish a strong market position, a credit union must gain credibility. A good way to position your credit union as an expert source of home mortgages is to conduct home-buyer educational seminars. Educating members is one of the fundamental purposes of credit unions, and expanding this service to the entire community provides an important public service. First-time buyers, in particular, need a reliable source of information. They are more likely to return to you for their home loans if you provided the information that helped them decide on homeownership or qualify for the loan. CUNA & Affiliates offers a Home Buying Program that includes a workbook and a thirty-minute video. These materials include advice on determining how much money is needed for a downpayment, preparing for the mortgage loan interview, comparison shopping for houses, and what to expect at the closing.

Providing consumer educational materials is another valuable service. These can be distributed not only in your lobby but also in libraries, schools, real estate offices, booths at community events, and on your web site. Again, this positions your credit union as an expert player in the mortgage business, and provides valuable information to the public.

Timing Is Everything

Woody Allen once observed that 90 percent of life is simply showing up. While establishing your credit union as a mortgage lender takes slightly more effort, "being there" does play a prominent role in market positioning. People shop for homes after work and on weekends. Lenders who can meet with applicants at the applicant's convenience, rather than the lender's, have the advantage. Having an application form on the web also allows twenty-four-hour access from virtually anywhere. Research suggests that it's critical to attract potential applicants while they are shopping around because once an application is submitted, few will drop it and start the process again with another lender.

Cross-Selling

A major benefit of mortgage lending is the opportunity for cross-selling other services. Mortgage loans are a core product, a product from which others can be generated. Effective cross-selling can bring new income sources and help position your credit union as your member's primary financial institution. Be aware that your competition is aggressively pursuing your members' mortgage business and the cross-selling opportunities it provides.

Use the Information

The mortgage loan application provides a great deal of information. The member discloses valuable data about spending and saving habits and product and service usage. How will your members know you want to be their primary financial institution if you don't ask for their business? Compare rates and conveniences and show them the many ways that the credit union offers a better deal. Build a relationship by packaging several products and services, including preapproving credit cards and credit lines, and presenting it along with the mortgage application.

If you offer direct deposit or Automated Clearing House (ACH) transactions for their mortgage payments, let your members know. Unless you tell them, many members may not know you offer these services. Cross-selling also requires active listening. Pay close attention to the member during the conversations that take place during the application process. Listen for unmet needs. That puts the credit union staff member in an ideal position to suggest services that meet those needs.

How will your members know that you want to be their primary financial institution if you don't ask for their business?

Mortgage lending opens the door to a wide range of opportunities for credit unions. A credit union with a closed field of membership has the option of serving its members by offering very limited services. It can thrive by doing an exceptional job in providing those few services. That option is not available to a community credit union. To succeed, it must operate as a full-service institution, and the simple truth is that a credit union that is not in the mortgage business cannot function as a full-service financial institution.

BUSINESS LENDING

Although they may appear to the casual observer as personal loans or home equity loans, many credit unions have loans on their books to members for business purposes. Business lending on a larger scale, however, has tended to be the domain of credit unions with $50 million or more in assets. A CUNA survey found that while overall some 12 percent of credit unions make business loans, 39 percent of credit unions with $50 to $199 million in assets do so. That percentage climbs to more than 45 percent for credit unions with $200 million or more in assets.

For community credit unions, business lending is a natural extension of their connection to the community. Charlie Grossklaus, president of Royal Credit Union in Eau Claire, Wisconsin, believes business lending is essential. "I don't think

---

community credit unions are going to survive without offering these loans," Grossklaus told *Credit Union Magazine.* "Credit unions have lost the new car loans, and the used-car market is increasingly competitive."

> *For community credit unions, business lending is a natural extension of their connection to the community.*

Grossklaus emphasizes that staying close to the business community and being involved in community projects are prerequisites. "We've had to be more involved with the communities we serve through industrial development programs, main street initiatives, and the chamber of commerce," he notes. Business lending has also allowed the credit union to expand its membership base and increase deposits and share draft accounts. Spreads are good on business loans, Grossklaus notes. By providing loans to the small-business owners that banks have snubbed, Royal accomplishes two goals. It not only supports the business community, but also provides many other services to its members—services it may not have been able to offer without the business loan income.

Business loans are not available to all comers, however. Regulations specify ineligible individuals, as identified in figure 8.2.

Figure 8.2 Business Loans: Not for Everyone

NCUA's Rules and Regulations Part 732.2 bar the following individuals from getting a member business loan:

- Your chief executive officer, president, or treasurer/manager
- Any assistant chief executive officers (for example, assistant president, vice president, or assistant treasurer/manager)
- Your chief financial officer (comptroller)
- Any family members of the people holding these positions

In addition, member business loans are disallowed if senior management employees, or any member of the board of directors who may be compensated as such, will benefit if the loan is approved.

BUSINESS LOANS DEFINED

As noted earlier, chances are that loans appear on the credit union's books that have been used to launch a business or shore up cash flow. Technically, they may not be defined as business loans. That definition can be found in NCUA's Rules and Regulations Part 723.1: "A member business loan includes any loan, line of credit, or letter of credit (including any unfunded commitments) where the borrower uses the proceeds for the following purposes:

1. Commercial;
2. Corporate;
3. Other business investment property or venture; or
4. Agricultural.

The rule also notes the following exceptions:

*   When a loan is fully secured by a lien on a one- to four-family dwelling that is the member's primary residence or by shares in the credit union making the extension of credit or deposits in other financial institutions.
*   When the loan or combination of loans obligated by one member is equal to or less than $50,000.
*   When the loan is guaranteed by a federal or state agency.
*   When a loan is granted by a corporate credit union to another credit union.

There are limits to business lending, too. Under NCUA's regulations, credit unions can have no more than 12.25 percent of assets in business loans. Individual business loans cannot exceed 15 percent of a credit union's net worth. A credit union can seek exemptions from these loan limits; in general, there are three ways to qualify:

*   Many community development or low-income-designated credit unions have obtained exemptions.
*   Credit unions chartered for the primary reason of making member business loans.
*   Credit unions that have a history of making primarily member business loans; at least 25 percent of loans are business loans, or member business loans make up the largest proportion of the portfolio.

Business lending provides a major growth opportunity for community credit unions. See figure 8.3 for specific advice on how to ensure that it provides a high quality asset.

Student Loans

With a price tag of between $30,000 to $77,000 for a four-year education, it's not surprising that half of all college students need help paying the bills. Education

Figure 8.3 Advice from the Front

Here are business lending tips gathered from credit union business lending veterans:

- Stay in compliance with your business loan policy. Have technology in place that allows you to track dollar amounts so that numbers can be reported to the board each month.

- Monitor your underwriting standards to ensure that they are keeping pace with current conditions. If a loan becomes delinquent, determine if your underwriting standards need adjustment, or if it's an isolated situation.

- Hire the expertise. Don't expect that you can turn the consumer lenders on your staff into agricultural or commercial lenders. Business lending requires special knowledge, skills, and an extensive network in the business community. You are most likely better off hiring that expertise than you are trying to retrain existing staff. In some cases, members of the business community will follow the person—whom they've come to know and trust—to the credit union.

- Stay tuned in. If appropriate, frequent the places of business where you've provided loans. Monitor economic trends affecting your trade area. Read the business section of the newspaper carefully.

- Details count. Follow evaluation and documentation procedures carefully, even on smaller loans. By not allowing any shortcuts, you set the tone for the process.

- Conduct site visits regularly and get the most recent financial data. Look for red flags such as aging account receivables, sagging sales, or surging expenses.

- Require the business to have its other accounts at the credit union. This not only cements the relationship, but also gives you a handle on the day-to-day cash flow.

loans not only provide a lending opportunity for credit unions, but also can establish a relationship with young members that brings future benefits. According to CUNA's Environmental Scan, most people choose their primary financial institution by the time they are twenty-five years old, and will stay with that institution for fifteen years.

Older members, too, may need education loans for themselves or their children. With insufficient savings, parents are turning to education loans to fill the gap. Federal loans to parents have risen substantially in recent years.

According to CUNA Mutual Business Services' Credit Union Student Loan Network, a federal initiative called the Master Promissory Note (MPN) makes it possible for students to remain with a single lender and servicer during their education and offers them a paper-free renewal process. In the past, an application for a Federal Stafford loan had to be filled out each year. The MPN is designed as either a single- or multiyear note; the choice is determined by the school. The MPN is valid for ten years from the date the note is signed by the borrower. It can be used for any loan disbursed within the ten-year lifetime as long as the first disbursement was issued within twelve months of the borrower's signature date.

"This feature is designed to encourage students to remain with one lender for all their student loans," notes Caroline Ashmore, product manager for the Student Loan Network, "and makes it critical for credit unions to market their student loan program to potential borrowers in their junior and senior year of high school." Students must be reached early, Ashmore cautions, because they only sign one MPN for all of their student loans throughout their education.

OPEN-END LENDING

As an open-end lending plan, the MPN is uniquely suited to the needs of students. But open-end plans are also attractive for reaching other segments of your membership. Multifeatured, open-end lending makes the loan process easier for both the member and the credit union. Because it minimizes the time it takes to underwrite a loan and streamlines the documentation process, it's ideal for the community credit union seeking to serve its members efficiently. Traditionally, credit unions have used open-end plans for lines of credit and overdraft protection. Now many are discovering the advantages of using these plans instead of closed-end loans for new or used vehicles, share-secured loans, certificate-secured loans—almost any consumer loan they normally make.

What Is Open-End Lending?

Open-end credit is defined in Regulation Z (12 CFR 226.2(a)(20) as, "Consumer credit extended by a creditor under a plan in which

- the creditor reasonably contemplates repeated transactions;
- the creditor may impose a finance charge from time to time on an outstanding unpaid balance; and
- the amount of credit that may be extended to the consumer during the term of the plan (up to any limit set by the creditor) is generally made available to the extent that any outstanding balance is repaid."

Therefore, to be considered open-end credit, the credit must be extended under a *plan* and must meet all three criteria of this definition. The credit union and the member execute a written agreement—the "plan" as defined in the regulation—in which both agree to an ongoing lending relationship. This is often called the Credit Agreement.

Using Subaccounts

By using subaccounts, the plan can be used to offer multiple types of credit. Each subaccount can have different rates, terms, and/or collateral. The requirement that the creditor "impose a finance charge from time to time on an outstanding unpaid balance" simply means that you must charge interest, but each subaccount can provide for different rates and terms.

Not all subaccounts under a plan need be used repeatedly or at all. For example, a subaccount for a new car is unlikely to be used repeatedly, and one for a recreational vehicle may never be used. The open-end plan, *as a whole*, must meet the definition of open-end credit, but each subaccount need not.

Credit unions' unique relationship with members provides the basis for meeting the plan requirement: "The creditor reasonably contemplates repeated transactions." It is your credit union's expectation that the plan will be reused, *not* the members' actual usage that determines whether the plan satisfies this requirement.

Advantages

Open-end credit plans can be used for secured lending as well as unsecured lending. They are particularly useful for car loans, because a member can be pre-approved for the maximum amount and use that preapproval when shopping for a vehicle. When he or she finds the right car, the credit union can finish the paper-work easily, including the security agreement.

The biggest advantage of using open-end plans is that the member need only apply and sign once for credit, when the plan is opened. The credit agreement is the umbrella that covers all loans under the plan, so once the member agrees to the plan's terms by signing it, there is never a reason to have another credit agreement signed. With a closed-end loan, a note must be signed each time the member borrows money. Truth-in-Lending initial disclosures must only be made once, when the plan is opened. With a closed-end loan, you must provide the disclosures every time—whether it's a loan for $100 or $10,000. There are fewer disclosures, too. While there are eighteen disclosures required for a closed-end loan, there are only four open-end disclosures to make.

Open-end credit also facilitates remote access to credit through the use of audio response systems, ATMs, call centers, kiosks, phone, or mail.

GETTING THE RIGHT MIX

The simple truth is that the cost of doing business is higher for community credit unions.

Your product and service menu determines to a large extent whether you can become a member's primary financial institution. And whether you are the PFI for a large segment of your members determines your profitability. The simple truth is that the cost of doing business is higher for community credit unions. Serving up the products and services that members want and need can go a long way to increase efficiencies. Implementing a multifeatured, open-end lending program also can reduce paperwork and streamline the lending process for both the member and the credit union.

REGULATORY OVERVIEW

Learner Objectives

Upon completion of this chapter, you will be able to

1. describe the general principles of a risk-based capital evaluation system; and

2. identify the wide range of rules and regulations with which your credit union must comply.

Community credit unions are not singled out for special regulations just because they are community credit unions. It just seems that way. Because of their complexity and the broad range of services they typically offer, such as mortgages and business loans, community credit unions may have a heavier regulatory burden than "plain vanilla" credit unions serving a single sponsor.

RISK-BASED CAPITAL

Most credit union people know that the Credit Union Membership Access Act allows credit unions to serve more people. Less well publicized is another directive. The fine print required that NCUA implement a risk-based capital evaluation system for "complex credit unions." Many community credit unions fit that description.

A risk-based capital system tends to provide a more accurate picture of a credit union's capital adequacy than does the capital-to-assets ratio rating system found in NCUA's CAMEL system. Briefly, a risk-based capital system weighs the riskiness of assets and compares these risk-weighted assets to a financial institution's capital categories. The system in use for banks includes both on-balance-sheet and off-balance-sheet risk and

- calculates several ratios of risk-weighted assets to capital to evaluate whether the institution is adequately capitalized;
- identifies levels of capital adequacy; and
- imposes limits and costs when it's determined the institution is inadequately capitalized.

RULES AND MORE RULES

Most regulations have been adopted to correct or prevent abuses. It's beyond the scope of this book to detail each and every law that affects community credit unions. In fact, with new regulations appearing every year, it's no wonder that from the perspective of many, "burdensome" is the most common adjective used to describe regulation. That said, regulatory compliance is a fact of life for credit unions.

From the perspective of many, "burdensome" is the most common adjective used to describe regulation.

What follows is a brief overview of the laws and regulations that may affect your credit union. It is neither comprehensive nor complete, only a starting point. For additional information, check the resources section of this book. Keep current by reading trade publications, particularly the "Compliance Matters" section of CUNA's *Credit Union Magazine*. CUNA also offers a "Regulatory Affairs" section on its web site, as well as an e-mail discussion group that serves as a forum for credit union participants to discuss their regulatory compliance concerns. To sign up, visit CUNA's web site at *www.cuna.org*; click on "Regulatory Affairs" then "COBWEB." COBWEB stands for Compliance Brainstorming on the Web. Also check out the "Reference Information" section of NCUA's web site (*www.ncua.gov*), for the complete text of its rules and regulations.

LENDING

- **Truth-in-Lending Act (Regulation Z)** standardizes how creditors' loan terms are disclosed and allows consumers to comparison shop. Truth-in-lending regulations apply differently to open-end and closed-end lending.

- **Fair Debt Collection Practices Act** sets the rules by which a debt collector can communicate with the debtor and other persons, and generally prohibits abusive collection practices.

- **The Equal Credit Opportunity Act (Regulation B)** promotes the availability of credit to all creditworthy applicants.

- **The Fair Credit Reporting Act** requires that if a loan or service is denied due to information contained in a credit report, the lender must disclose to the applicant, the name, address, and telephone number of the source.

- **The Fair Credit Billing Act** specifies loss limits for lost or stolen credit cards, and procedures for correcting errors and settling disputed charges. **Holder in due course** provides remedies for consumers who experience problems with the quality of products or services purchased with a credit card.

- **The Fair Housing Act** prohibits discrimination in the sale or rental of residential property, requires the conspicuous display of an Equal Housing Lender poster, and prescribes what can be included in any printed advertisement.

- **The National Flood Insurance Reform Act** requires applicants to buy and maintain flood insurance if a property is located in a special flood hazard area.

- **The Real Estate Settlement Procedures Act (RESPA)** requires lenders to provide mortgage loan applicants with disclosures relating to settlement costs, and governs the treatment of escrow/impound-held funds for the payment of taxes and insurance premiums.

- **The Financial Institutions Reform Recovery and Enforcement Act of 1989 (FIRREA)** requires NCUA to set regulations for using state certified or licensed appraisers in federally related transactions. These rules are defined in NCUA Regulations Part 722.

- **The Home Mortgage Disclosure Act (HMDA)** requires a credit union to complete and submit to NCUA yearly HMDA data about loan applications received for home purchases or home improvements; loans originated; and loans purchased if, on the prior December 31, the credit union had assets of more than $28 million *and* a home or branch office in a metropolitan statistical area or in a primary metropolitan statistical area.

- **NCUA Lending Rules and Regulations** of special note include the following:

    Mortgage Lending:

    NCUA Letter No. 124 to Credit Unions

    NCUA Letter No. 154 to Credit Unions

    NCUA Letter 99-12

    Member Business Loans:

    12 CFR Parts 701, 722, 723, and 741

In addition, your credit union must comply with any applicable state rules—for example, regulations regarding real estate transactions.

SHARES AND TRANSACTIONS

- **Truth-in-Savings (Regulation DD)** requires financial institutions to disclose fully and clearly the fees and terms of their deposit accounts. Rates must be quoted in terms of annual percentage yield, and this must be disclosed in advertising. Part 707 of NCUA Rules and Regulations implements Truth-in-Savings for federal credit unions and federally insured, state-chartered credit unions.

- **Expedited Funds Availability Act (Regulation CC)** specifies how long checks can be "held" and requires disclosure of the financial institution's practices.

- **Electronic Funds Transfer Act (Regulation E)** sets the basic rights, responsibilities, and liabilities of consumers and institutions regarding electronic funds transfer services.

- **Federal Reserve Regulation J** addresses all electronic funds transfers not subject to Regulation E, including all wire transfers.

- **Regulation D** sets monetary reserve requirements that covered institutions must maintain at the Federal Reserve.

- **Regulation M** requires meaningful disclosures of leasing terms.

- **The Debt Collection Improvement Act** mandates that all federal payments except tax refunds be made electronically.

Various rules and reporting requirements from the **Internal Revenue Service** also affect credit unions, as do applicable state laws. Finally, the following laws are in effect: **Bank Secrecy Act, Right to Financial Privacy Act,** and **Bank Bribery Act.**

While at times it may seem as though your credit union is drowning in an alphabet soup of regulations, keep in mind that help is available from a wide range of sources: books, materials, publications, schools, and conferences from your league, CUNA, and other trade groups, including the National Association of Community Credit Unions, and yes, even your regulator.

INSURANCE PROTECTION

You also can purchase insurance coverage. Supplemental litigation coverage, for example, can protect the credit union from certain claims alleging the following:

- A breach of contract or agreement with its members
- Wrongful repossession of property or wrongful disclosure
- Unintentional error or omission in payment of shares or deposits, or in application of funds received from a member
- Unintentional violation of the U.S. Bankruptcy Code, the Fair Debt Collection Practices Act, or any similar federal, state, or local statute, law, rule or regulation
- Unintentional violation of any unfair or deceptive trade practices act
- Error or omission based solely on the credit union's status as a lienholder or secured party

Usually, this insurance is part of a special package that also includes a Directors, Volunteers and Employees (DVE) policy. The DVE protects credit union directors, volunteers, and employees from lawsuits arising out of their duties performed for the credit union. Examples include breach of duty, negligence, misstatement, and misleading statements. This policy, for example, provides coverage, within policy limits, for a credit union employee who, in error, fails to provide the necessary disclosures to a member applying for a loan and is subsequently sued by the member for negligence. Credit unions also can purchase a "Consumer Legislation" endorsement to their bond coverage to protect against losses due to violation of consumer laws.

Think of insurance protection as a safety net, not as a license to disregard rules and regulations willfully—just as it makes no sense to drive recklessly because you have auto coverage or to leave unattended food cooking on a stove because you have homeowner's insurance.

Think of insurance protection as a safety net, not as a license to disregard rules and regulations willfully.

BOARD INVOLVEMENT

Management must keep the board of directors fully informed about regulations and bring any needed policy changes to the board's attention. There is an apocryphal story in the credit union industry that goes like this: Management presents a full description of the provisions of the Truth-in-Lending Act as implemented by Regulation Z, only to have the board of directors vote not to follow it. While this story may only be credit union myth, it points to the need for an engaged board that recognizes its obligations. Board members should be urged to attend all board meetings, as directors are liable for what boards do or don't do, whether or not they attend the meetings. Part of every board meeting agenda should include time for director education on the prevailing laws. Directors must be aware that the violation of many laws can result in litigation against them personally.

STAY KNOWLEDGEABLE

Don't be overwhelmed by the sheer number of regulations your credit union must adhere to. But don't ignore them either. Keep policies and procedures in place that are in compliance, and seek legal counsel when you are uncertain of your course of action. Keep abreast of changes. Insure against losses you are unable to absorb internally.

GLOSSARY

Affinity A relationship upon which a community charter is based. NCUA defines acceptable affinities as living, working, worshiping, or attending school in a community.

Appeal The right of a credit union or charter applicant to request that the National Credit Union Administration Board formally review a regional director's adverse decision.

Business plan Plan submitted by a charter applicant or existing credit union specifying the economic advisability of a proposed charter or field of membership addition.

Call center A telephone/data processing system that handles member inquiries. May include having the capability to accept and approve loan applications.

Charter The document authorizing a group to operate as a credit union. It defines the limits of its operating authority, generally including the persons the credit union can accept for membership. The National Credit Union Administration issues charters for federal credit unions. The designated state chartering authority does so for credit unions organized under the laws of that state.

Common bond The characteristic or combination of characteristics that distinguishes a particular group of people from the general public. There are two common bonds that serve as a basis for a group forming a federal credit union or being included in an existing federal credit union's field of membership: occupational—employment by the same company or related companies—and associational—membership in the same association.

Community credit union A credit union whose field of membership consists of people who live, work, worship, or attend school in the same well-defined local community, neighborhood, or rural district.

Credit union A member-owned, not-for-profit cooperative financial institution formed to permit those in the field of membership specified in the charter to save, borrow, and obtain related financial services.

Economic advisability An overall evaluation of the credit union's or charter applicant's ability to operate successfully.

Emergency merger Pursuant to section 205(h) of the Federal Credit Union Act, the authority of NCUA to merge two credit unions without regard to common bond policy.

Exclusionary clause A limitation, written in a credit union's charter, that precludes the credit union from serving a portion of a group which otherwise could be included in its field of membership. Exclusionary clauses are used to prevent certain overlaps of fields of membership between credit unions.

Federal share insurance Insurance coverage provided by the National Credit Union Share Insurance Fund and administered by the National Credit Union Administration. Coverage is provided for qualified accounts in all federal credit unions and state credit unions with federal insurance.

Field of membership The people, organizations, and other legal entities, a credit union can accept for membership.

Household People living in the same residence maintaining a single economic unit.

Immediate family member A spouse, child, sibling, parent, grandparent, or grandchild. This includes stepparents, stepchildren, stepsiblings, and adoptive relationships.

Letter of Understanding and Agreement Agreement between NCUA and federal credit union officials not to engage in certain activities and/or to establish reasonable operational goals. Typically, new charter applicants must enter into this agreement for a limited time.

Low-income credit union A low-income credit union is defined in section 701.34 of the NCUA Rules and Regulations as one in which a majority of its members either earn less than 80 percent of the average for all wage earners as established by the Bureau of Labor Statistics, or whose annual household income falls at or below 80 percent of the median household income for the nation. The term *low income* also includes members who are full-time or part-time students in a college, university, high school, or vocational school.

Metropolitan area A large population nucleus, together with adjacent communities having a high degree of social and economic integration with that core. Metropolitan areas make up one or more entire counties, except in New England, where cities and towns are the basic geographic units. The Office of Management and Budget defines metropolitan areas for purposes of collecting, tabulating, and publishing federal data. Metropolitan area definitions result from applying published standards to Census Bureau data.

Merger Absorption by one credit union of all the assets, liabilities, and equity of another credit union. The National Credit Union Administration and the appropriate state regulator, if a state credit union is involved, must approve the merger.

Multiple common bond credit union A credit union whose field of membership consists of more than one group, each of which has a common bond of occupation or association.

National Association of Community Credit Unions NACCU is a professional network of community credit union staff and directors that supports the mission of community credit unions. NACCU seeks to share educational information and help provide solutions to fellow community credit unions.

National Credit Union Administration NCUA is the federal regulator, governed by a three-member board appointed by the President and confirmed by the Senate.

Occupational common bond Employment by the same entity or related entities.

Once a member, always a member A provision of the Federal Credit Union Act that permits an individual to remain a member of the credit union until he or she chooses to withdraw or is expelled. Under this provision, leaving a group specified in the credit union's charter does not end an individual's membership in the credit union.

Overlap The situation that results when a group is eligible for membership in more than one credit union.

Plain vanilla A term often used to describe credit unions that offer only loans and shares.

Purchase and assumption Purchase of all or part of the assets of and assumption of all or part of the liabilities of one credit union by another credit union. The purchased and assumed credit union must first be placed into involuntary liquidation.

Service area The area that can reasonably be served by the service facilities accessible to the groups within the field of membership.

Service facility A place where loan applications and shares are accepted, and loans are dispersed.

Single common bond credit union A credit union whose field of membership consists of one group with a common bond of occupation or association.

Single occupational common bond credit union A credit union whose field of membership consists of employees of the same entity or related entities.

Spin-off The transfer of a portion of the field of membership, assets, liabilities, shares, and capital of one credit union to a new or existing credit union.

Subscribers For a federal credit union, at least seven individuals who sign the charter application and pledge at least one share.

Underserved community A local community, neighborhood, or rural district that is an "investment area" as defined in section 103(16) of the Community Development Banking and Financial Institutions Act of 1994. The area must also be underserved based on other NCUA and federal banking agency data.

Unsafe or unsound practice Any action, or lack of action, that would result in an abnormal risk or loss to the credit union, its members, or the National Credit Union Share Insurance Fund.

INDEX

frequently asked questions, *60*
"fringe bankers," 23

G

geography, 10
goodwill, 36

H

Heartland Credit Union, 55, 72
holder in due course, 91
home-buyer seminars, 80–81
home financial services, 69–71
Home Mortgage Disclosure Act, 16, 91–92
household incomes, *15, 22*
households, 12–13

I

image
    communicating, 34–39
    feedback about, 31–33
    importance of, 30–31
    profiling current, 33–34
    protecting, 39
immediate family members, 12, 13–14
incomes, *15, 22*
in-store branches, 72–73
insurance, 93–94
interactive voice response systems, 74
International Credit Union Operating
    Principles, 41
Internet-based systems, 70–71, 79
IRPS-99, 9, 10–11, *12*

J

John Deere Community Credit Union, 39

K

kiosks, 72

L

La Caisse Populaire de Lévis, 3
La Caisse Populaire Ste. Marie, 4

lending policies, 26–28
lending regulations, 91–92
lifeline banking, 24
litigation insurance, 93–94
local community requirement, 10
location, 67–68, 71–72
lower-income households, 23–25, 26–28

M

management reorganization, 58–59
maps, *12*
marketing
    about charter conversions, 61–62
    of image, 34–39
    of product mix, 78, 79–82
Master Promissory Note, 86
media, 38, *80*
median income, 22
medical bills, 28
membership
    early limits on, 5
    legislation about, 5–6, 9
    listening to, 32
    reasons for, 29–30
    See also field of membership
mergers, 54–55
Metro Federal Credit Union, 13–14
metropolitan areas, *15,* 16
minibranches, 73
mortgages, 78–82, 91–92

N

name changes, 59–60, 61–62
National Credit Union Administration
    (NCUA)
    community charter requirements, 10–11
    field of membership issues and, 5
    lending regulations of, 92
National Flood Insurance Reform Act, 91
needs surveys, 43–46
nominating committees, 56–57
nonmember deposits, 17
Novi Community Credit Union, 38–39

O

P

R

S

T

timeline of credit union history, *2*
transaction account regulations, 92
trust, 30–31
Truth-in-Lending Act, 91
Truth-in-Savings, 92

U

underserved areas, serving, 14–16. *See also* lower-income households
unemployment, *15*

V

virtual branches, 69–71
voice response systems, 74
volunteering. *See* community relations

W

Web services, 70–71, 79

BOOKS

Branch Operations Ready Reference, #21226-JK1

A valuable resource for managers and other involved staff. Chapters include information on leadership for branch managers, motivating and coaching employees, managing a sales culture, regulatory compliance, branch efficiency, financial counseling, cash management, productivity reporting, strategic planning, and electronic delivery of services. $45.95, 1999

Catch Members with the Net: A Guide to Maximizing Web Site Effectiveness, #22261-JK1

Is it the right time for your credit union to join Internet commerce? Can you create a web site yourself or do you need to outsource it? What about maintenance and staffing issues? These and other questions are answered in this handbook. Also discussed are the history, rationale, and uses of a web site, and the key concerns of maintaining and analyzing web site effectiveness. Learn about the important part that marketing plays in web site effectiveness and

- Basic web site design
- Site security
- Legal issues
- High-quality and fresh content and design
- Web site effectiveness tracking
- Web site marketing
- The future of the World Wide Web

Also included are sample web sites, basic HTML instruction, a sample worksheet, and checklists. Web sites are becoming an integral part of credit union operations and marketing efforts. $34.95, 1999

Credit Union Call Center Handbook, #22259-JK1

Here's a concise guide to develop, implement, and evaluate a credit union call center. Designed to explore critical issues in call center development, operations, and management, this handbook provides valuable insights into the major components of the call center environment and will save you time and money.

The *Credit Union Call Center Handbook* covers

- Call center background, objectives, transactions, and marketing
- Call center technology applications and integration
- Cost-benefit considerations
- Call processing and procedures development
- Staffing
- Burnout prevention and coaching

Appendices provide call center statistics, procedure and observation forms, performance standards, business plan, a glossary, and resources. $29.95, 1999

Credit Union Mortgage Lending Strategies: The Best Never Rest, #22639-JK1

Here's a book for those who are ready to do mortgage lending in a serious way. This resource is not a how-to-get-started approach, but "stage two" for credit union leadership and management. *Credit Union Mortgage Lending Strategies* is for those who are out of the gate and need to know the trends and influences. It looks at key issues and strategic decision making. Readable and stimulating, this book also includes case studies based on actual credit union experiences. In this dynamic area, this is the *one* book that informs, motivates, and guides credit union managers to build and run a competitive program successfully. $39.95, 2000

Online Laws and Regulations for Credit Unions: Internet Legal Implications, #22561-JK1

Become familiar with the laws and regulations that credit unions must follow to catch the growing wave of Internet commerce. This book includes specific examples of how those regulations apply and the consequences of noncompliance. In each chapter, the laws and regulations covered are listed as subject areas within the chapter, making it easy for you to find information about a particular law or rule. *Online Laws and Regulations* includes a glossary of Internet terms and a reprint of an NCUA Regulatory Alert containing NCUA's opinion on many of the compliance issues that arise in Internet transactions. $34.95, 1999

Technocasting for Credit Unions: Identifying Tomorrow's Technology Needs Today, #22260-JK1

Learn to use a "business-first" approach when making technology decisions. Discover the most compelling technology options available in the financial industry today. And learn how to take a systematic approach to your credit union technology decisions. *Technocasting for Credit Unions* covers new and upcoming technologies, the potential and pitfalls of the World Wide Web, budgeting for and analyzing the performance of technology, and more! $34.95, 1999

To order, call CUNA Customer Service at (800) 356-8010, ext. 4157, or use the order form at the back of this handbook.

Sharing the American Dream, Credit Union Executives Society, Madison, Wisconsin, 1986. For information call (608) 288-5300.

WHITE PAPERS

Brick and Mortar versus Technology, National Association of Community Credit Unions, 1999.

Converting to a Community Charter, National Association of Community Credit Unions, 2000.

For information call (800) 356-9655, ext. 4033.

CERTIFICATE PROGRAMS

STAR (Staff Training and Recognition)

STAR S600, *Credit Union Technology*

This module provides an overview of the types of technology credit unions use—ATMs, debit and credit cards, ACH, call centers, home financial services, web sites—and the staff's role in providing these services. From the members' vantage point, the frontline staff is the credit union. This module helps frontline staff understand credit union technology and how it is used.

STAR S610, *Working with Technology*

This module explains the various technologies used in credit unions along with staff responsibilities. Chapter headings include transactions via remote terminals, communication systems, telephone transactions, PC transactions, and support systems. Regulation E is also covered, including: purpose of the regulation; types of electronic services covered by Reg E; exemptions, disclosures, error resolution procedures; and member liability. The final chapter provides strategies for individual employees to adapt and learn new technologies.

STAR S620, *Serving Members with Technology*

Although members expect the latest in technology, they still expect the personal service that credit unions provide. This module helps staff provide the human dimension to technology, which is so frequently missing. It offers examples from leading credit unions that have successfully combined technology with effective member service.

MERIT (Management Training and Recognition)

M17, *Credit Union Financial Management for Nonfinancial Executives*

Here's an efficient overview of credit union financial operations. This easy-to-understand module includes information on capital adequacy, asset-liability management, cash-flow forecasting, spread analysis, and ratio analysis. Learn about balance sheets, income statements, and risk management.

M20, *Managing Technology*

In this fast-changing world, effective strategic planning seems to require a magical ability to predict tomorrow's technology. While that may be impossible, what *is* required is an ability to be fast on your feet in reacting to new technologies as they become available. Understanding these technological opportunities and dealing with the rapid rate of introduction are topics covered in *Managing Technology*. Through six chapters, the author discusses the role of technology, perspectives on financial service technology, the role of management, working with the staff, and controlling electronic fraud. Also included are suggested resources on technology topics.

M29, *Providing Loans to Small Businesses*

This course will help you gain proficiency in this emerging area of credit union growth. Includes details on documentation for processing, small business administration, asset-liability strategies, decision making, and monitoring underwriting standards.

M31, *Budgeting and Accounting for Nonaccounting Managers*

This course takes you through the accounting process step-by-step, providing an overview of the basics. You also learn about closing accounts, accounting systems, asset accounting, liabilities, shares and reserves, budgeting, and planning.

VAP (Volunteer Achievement Program)

V500, *Credit Union Technology*

Gain an understanding of the basic technology components and directors' roles in oversight. Includes information on the delivery systems, back office systems, and the Internet.

V501, *Planning for Technology*

Learn basic principles of planning for successful technology. Includes information on board and management roles, competitive demands of technology, how technology affects people, developing effective policies, and achieving member satisfaction.

V502, *Electronic Fraud and Security*

Gives directors an understanding of electronic fraud and security issues. Includes an overview of preventive and detection technologies. Focuses on implementing security measures while meeting members' needs. Relevant laws and regulations are also covered.

V600, *Introduction to Mortgage Lending*

This module is written for credit union directors and other volunteers who have responsibilities for oversight of mortgage lending. It's also designed for credit unions where leaders are considering whether to develop a mortgage program. Includes a general discussion of credit union mortgage lending programs, and why such programs are increasingly important. It looks at mortgage lending risks, terminology, getting a program started, marketing, regulations, and types of loan products.

V601, *Online Policies and Internet Use*

Board and management policies need to maximize the benefits of e-mail and Internet access while controlling the risks. This module acquaints directors with the potential risks and policy implications of staff use of the Internet and e-mail. It will help directors ask the right questions of management and guide them in establishing policies.

Chapters cover the basics of computers and computer networking, potential problems and risks associated with e-mail and the Internet, the drafting and communication of policy, some technology related to risk control, and an overview of regulations and laws affecting credit union Internet use. Appendices give examples of sample policies and a checklist for their formation, an article on Internet etiquette, and a glossary of computer and Internet terms.

To order these STAR, MERIT, or VAP products, contact your state league.

VIDEOS

Planning for Technology: Planning for Change Video, CUTV149-JK1

This video shows you how other credit unions have used technology to create opportunities to provide better service to their members. Designed as a decision-making tool, this video takes you behind the scenes to see and hear how credit union CEOs and managers have successfully worked through the issues surrounding the planning and implementation of new technology. They'll share with you the successes and failures of technology integration. More than a planning tool, this video will help you make informed decisions. Length: 21 minutes, $138.00

Planning for Technology: Planning for People Video, CUTV150-JK1

Learn about the people part of the relationship between technology and members. This video offers insights from CEOs and managers at credit unions that are blazing new trails. These individuals share the successes and failures of technology implementation from firsthand experience. Topics include how to build a people plan to fit your technology plan, how to avoid the negative impact of technology on day-to-day operations, how to raise the technology comfort level of staff, and how and when to outsource technical training for staff. Length: 29:42 minutes, $138.00

1999–2000 Environmental Scan Video, #30006-JK1

The E-Scan video provides information about current issues and forces shaping the financial world. Using a news format, this video gives viewers a concise overview of the information contained in the Environmental Scan report. Length: approx. 31 minutes, $135.00

Prices subject to change based on reprints and revisions.

WEB SITES

CUNA Mutual. "Access SCAM Alerts." 1999. SCAM alert is a fraud awareness program sponsored by CUNA Mutual Group. Its goal is to provide frontline credit union personnel with pertinent information on current fraudulent schemes. *www.cunamutual.com/common/scamprog.html*

National Federation of Community Development Credit Unions. This site contains basic information on CDCUs and the federation, and includes links to other development resources and the credit union movement. *www.natfed.org*

ORGANIZATIONS

National Association of Community Credit Unions, a professional network of community credit union staff and directors that supports the mission of community credit unions. NACCU is designed to share educational information and help provide solutions to fellow community credit unions. Web site is available at *www.cuna.org;* click on "community credit unions."

Credit Union Board of Directors Handbook, #22824-JK1
Third Edition

Helps your directors build confidence and gain shared understandings which lead to a united, purposeful board. Provides information on: board of directors profile—legal liabilities; conflict of interest; government oversight; insurance protection; becoming an effective director; duties and responsibilities; board's role in relation to other committees and staff; how to establish and maintain a good relationship with your credit union's chief executive officer; how to improve communications with members, management, and committees.

152 pages $24.95   1999

Credit Union Call Center Handbook, #22259-JK1

Guides you through the development, implementation, and evaluation of a credit union call center, and explores critical issues in development, operations, and management. Covers call center background, objectives, transactions and marketing, technology applications and integration, cost-benefit considerations, call processing and procedures development, staffing, burnout prevention, and coaching. Appendices provide call center statistics, procedure and observation forms, performance standards, and a business plan.

117 pages $29.95   1999

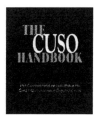

The CUSO Handbook, #22267-JK1

Credit Union Service Organizations offer a unique opportunity to do more for members. CUSOs have proven their value by enabling credit unions to enhance member services, rein in operational costs, and develop new partnerships. This book explores the variety and versatility offered by the CUSO structure, along with legal and operational issues. Also covers using a CUSO to do more for members, effectively organizing a CUSO, meeting legal and regulatory requirements, creating member services and operational CUSO opportunities, applying business planning principles, and learning from the experiences of successful CUSOs.

151 pages $29.95   1999

Director's Handbook for Credit Union Examinations, #21782-JK1

This handbook helps directors understand the NCUA examination process, examiner concerns, and examination preparation. Chapters include overview of the exam process, director and management preparation, on-site examination scope, CAMEL rating system, and the joint conference and examination report. Also included are relevant NCUA documents, checklists, and examples of problems as well as strategies to remedy these problems.

128 pages $29.95   1999

Director's Handbook for Credit Union Regulations, #21310-JK1

The more directors know about the laws and regulations that govern credit unions, the better they can perform their jobs. This handbook gives directors the regulatory information they need in a style that is easy to read and fast paced. Chapters cover the laws and regulations affecting credit unions, rules for the organizational structure of federal credit unions, regulatory requirements associated with maintaining federal share insurance, consumer protection regulations and laws governing credit union operations, general lending regulations, including NCUA and Federal Reserve Board regulations, and information on additional resources.

128 pages $29.95   1999

Credit Union Marketing Handbook, #21253-JK1

Effective marketing powers successful organizations. Because of the special relationship credit unions have with members, marketing to both current and potential members is especially critical. You'll learn how to: develop marketing strategies for new and existing products, use distribution systems—both direct and indirect—effectively, use advertising, public relations, and sales promotion, develop pricing strategies to ensure growth while fulfilling your mission, formulate marketing objectives and goals, project sales, calculate the return on a marketing investment in order to track results, develop and manage the marketing process, and write a marketing plan. The appendix includes a marketing plan format.

166 pages $29.95   1998

Credit Union Political Action Handbook, #21305-JK1

Helps guide your credit union in effective political action at local, state, and national levels. Everyone who has the responsibility for safeguarding the future of our credit unions should read this handbook. This includes directors, volunteers, managers, marketers, and staff who handle communications, legislative, or political activities. Beginning with an introduction to the political process, the handbook rapidly moves to describe credit unions in relation to politics, elections, and legislation. It provides case studies in the areas of political process and lobbying. It will help your credit union create and maintain a consistent political presence, rather than rallying efforts only in time of crisis.

109 pages $29.95   1998

Credit Union Supervisory Committee Handbook, #763-JK1
Second Edition

Helps committee members succeed by giving them information on supervisory committee profile qualifications; makeup of the committee; removal from the committee; legal considerations; insurance protection; conflict of interest; duties and responsibilities; supervisory committee relationships—with members, directors, other committee members, management and staff, external and internal auditors, and your regulatory agency.

130 pages $14.95   1997

Volunteers and Lending, #21222-JK1

Offers a contemporary view of lending trends, committee roles, and the issues facing credit union lenders. Looks at the market forces that are causing credit committees to change, be replaced, or be eliminated entirely. Even though committees are changing, directors and volunteers still have responsibility for sound lending policies and practices. These important duties are outlined, with information and guidelines provided for various positions.

112 pages $29.95   1998

Managing Staff Recruitment: How to Hire the Best and the Brightest, #22258-JK1

Covers relevant employment laws, policies and procedures, job advertisements, preliminary screening, interviewing, and final selection. Also covers
- understanding today's employment environment;
- attracting skilled people;
- recruiting techniques;
- identifying qualified candidates;
- interviewing effectively;
- providing employee orientation.

Your employees are your most valuable resource. *Managing Staff Recruitment* helps you retain a dedicated, long-term work force. Includes sample job application, interview guide, self-evaluation, job descriptions, and more!

181 pages $34.95   1999

Catch Members with the Net: A Guide to Maximizing Web Site Effectiveness, #22261-JK1

This handbook discusses the history, rationale, and uses of a web site, and the key concerns of maintaining and analyzing web site effectiveness. Includes:

- basic web site design;
- security and legal issues;
- keeping your content and design fresh;
- tracking your web site's effectiveness;
- marketing your site.

Also included are sample web sites, basic HTML instruction, a sample worksheet, and checklists. Web sites are becoming an integral part of credit union operations and marketing efforts. Learn how to create an effective site for your credit union!

150 pages $34.95   1999

Technocasting for Credit Unions: Identifying Tomorrow's Technology Needs Today, #22260-JK1

Discover the most compelling technology options available in the financial industry today, and learn how to take a systematic approach for your credit union technology decisions. Topics include:

- forecasting and planning for technology;
- new and upcoming technologies;
- possibilities and pitfalls of the World Wide Web;
- budgeting for and analyzing performance of technology;
- technology staffing and implementation;
- technology vendors.

Use *Technocasting for Credit Unions* as your credit union resource for making technology decisions. Feel confident that you're using technology to help members take control of their financial lives.

131 pages $34.95   1999

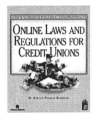

Online Laws and Regulations for Credit Unions: Internet Legal Implications, #22561-JK1

Explores the laws and regulations credit unions must follow in catching the growing wave of Internet commerce. Includes specific examples of how those regulations apply and the consequences of noncompliance. *Online Laws and Regulations* also covers:

- general legal principles;
- compliance issues;
- new accounts;
- lending over the Internet;
- electronic funds transfers;
- privacy and security concerns.

Includes a glossary of Internet terms and a reprint of an NCUA *Regulatory Alert* containing the NCUA's opinion on many of the compliance issues that arise in Internet transactions.

120 pages $34.95   1999

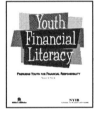

Youth Financial Literacy: Preparing Youth for Financial Responsibility, #22646-JK1

Offers suggestions for developing formal financial curricula in schools; building community awareness of the need for financial education; and getting parents, educators, administrators, and students involved in the process. Youth Financial Literacy also covers

- developing highly focused relationships with youth;
- strengthening relationships with parents;
- providing training seminars for youth and parents;
- building rapport with school systems;
- becoming involved in community programs for youth;
- preparing Internet pages to educate youth;
- developing a youth program as part of the credit union's overall objectives and goals.

Illustrates how easy it is to develop savings, investment, lending, share draft, and other programs for youth, and provides case studies of specific credit unions' youth programs, classroom presentations, community activities, seminars, and special promotions.

147 pages $29.95   1999

An Intro to MCIF: How Marketing Customer Information Files Can Benefit Your Credit Union, #22624-JK1

The MCIF is a powerful marketing and technological tool. It can help your credit union increase its membership, increase members' use of the credit union's products and services, and improve the credit union's financial performance. This handbook will help credit unions understand the MCIF and use it effectively. Includes:

- identifying MCIF alternatives;
- choosing the right MCIF alternatives;
- choosing the right MCIF solution for your credit union;
- understanding standard MCIF operations;
- learning how credit unions use MCIFs in marketing and strategic initiatives.

Also included are case studies, worksheets for comparing MCIF providers, and statistics from a survey of CUNA Marketing Council members on their use of MCIFs.

85 pages $34.95   1999

Marketing Across the Generations: Youth, Ages 0–19, #22900-JK1

Today's children and teenagers possess spending—and saving—power unparalleled in previous generations. Marketing to this group produces high-revenue, long-term relationships with low-risk members. This handbook, part of a four-part series, covers

- designing effective products and promotions for the material generation;
- communicating effectively without falling into the "cool" trap;
- developing saving clubs, youth branches, and education programs;
- managing the transition from youth to adult member;
- measuring the effectiveness of your youth marketing efforts.

Short "Snapshots" describe exemplary youth marketing programs, and "Credit Union Action Steps" at the end of each chapter offer suggestions to put the strategies presented in the handbook to work at your credit union.

136 pages $29.95   2000

Marketing Across the Generations: Generation X, Ages 20–35, #22899-JK1

For many credit unions, identifying with generation X has become a critical factor as they make their long-range plans and position themselves for the twenty-first century. This handbook is one in a four-part series devoted to marketing to various age groups. It explores numerous issues relating to the generation X market segment.

This handbook helps credit unions develop programs targeted to generation X members ages twenty to thirty-five. It includes educational and informational programs as well as services that will attract these members. The handbook also provides methods for communicating with generation X and case studies of successful marketing. It also covers

- age ranges used in defining generation X;
- characteristics, statistical, and demographic information;
- specific marketing issues and practical ways to reach gen Xers;
- E-commerce, Internet, and other technologies;
- the values and appeal of credit unions to generation X;
- the future forecast for generation X.

114 pages $29.95   2000

Marketing Across the Generations: Baby Boomers, Ages 35–53, #22898-JK1

Boomers are a large, diverse, and profitable market segment for credit unions. This handbook—one in a series of four—helps you understand the sheer size of this group and the statistical implications for your credit union over the next forty years. The handbook also includes information on

- examining which credit union products offer the greatest appeal to baby boomers, and why;
- developing promotional and product ideas for the boomer market;
- providing additional services for individuals approaching their golden years;
- realizing the promotional and cross-selling opportunities of the Internet;
- assisting baby boomers with their saving, investing, and retirement planning needs;
- offering and marketing mortgage loan programs;
- becoming a one-stop financial center for boomer members.

"Credit Union Action Steps" help you put plans into action. Examples from experienced, frontline marketers illustrate promotional strategies that appeal to boomers. While difficult to pigeonhole, baby boomers represent an upscale, high-interest-paying market segment. The handbook helps you serve this profitable group.
$29.95   2000

Marketing Across the Generations: Fifty-plus, Ages 50 and Above, #22897-JK1

Many financial marketers make the mistake of viewing the fifty-plus segment as one mass market. Actually, this group is as diverse as the others covered in this four-part series on generational marketing. The needs of an actively employed fifty-year-old are quite different from those of a seventy-year-old retiree. And individuals in record numbers are living healthy, productive lives into their eighties, nineties, and beyond. This handbook covers information on

- examining the various life stages that can occur in the fifties and beyond;
- providing convenience for members who are no longer linked to a workplace;
- offering loans geared to older members;
- maintaining relationships with loyal members who truly believe in the credit union philosophy;
- preparing a detailed marketing plan to carry out core strategies;
- offering educational presentations and opportunities for the fifty-plus market.

Also included are ideas for creating and maintaining a "Seniors Club." Marketing to mature ages and life stages is undergoing dramatic change because of technology, longer life spans, and other factors. This handbook shows how to take advantage of these new and expanded opportunities for marketing to the fifty-plus segment. "Credit Union Action Steps" and case studies lead the way.
$29.95   2000

Credit Union Mortgage Lending Strategies: The Best Never Rest, #22639-JK1

Here's a book for those who are ready to do mortgage lending in a serious way. Not a how-to-get-started approach, this is stage two for credit union leadership and management—for those who need to know the trends and influences. It looks at key issues and strategic decision-making and includes case studies based on actual credit union experiences. Sections include

- The Credit Union Mortgage Lending Environment;
- Doing the Right Things Right;
- Mortgage Marketing Strategies;
- Beyond Tradition.

A successful, sustained mortgage lending program involves many challenges. *Credit Union Mortgage Lending Strategies* is the one book that motivates and guides executives, managers, and directors to build and run competitive programs.
136 pages $39.95   2000

Credit Union Branding: Winning Strategies for Marketers, #22640-JK1

Provides the tools you need to meet the challenges of brand marketing. By giving brands distinctive qualities, brand marketers create loyalty for their products and services, and their credit unions. Provides a comprehensive background on the history, strategy, and opportunities of brand marketing. Includes

- the lexicon of branding;
- functional and emotional benefits of brands;
- tactics for implementing a brand marketing program;
- trademark protection;
- brand consistency and revitalization;
- examples of great branding techniques.

Also included is information on the National Credit Union Brand Campaign. Learn how you can effectively manage your credit union brand!
122 pages $34.95   1999

To place an order or ask a question:

Call **1-800-356-8010, press 3**
(or dial ext. 4157)
7:30 a.m. to 6:00 p.m.
Monday–Friday, CST
Local calls 608-231-4157
TTY phone 1-800-356-8030

Fax 1-608-231-1869

Mail the order form to:
CUNA Customer Service
P.O. Box 333
Madison, WI 53701–0333

E-Mail customerservice@cuna.com

CUNA & Affiliates Order Form

Ship to:

Credit union

Attention

Street address for shipping

City/State/Zip

Bill to:

Credit union

Attention   Title

Address

City/State/Zip

Phone   Ext. #

Fax

Payment method

☐ Credit unions in U.S.:
No need to prepay, we'll bill you for the total amount of your order.

☐ Individuals and International customers:
Must prepay in U.S. dollars.

Quantity	Stock Number	Description	Unit Price	Total

Subtotal: We'll calculate the freight and handling (plus sales tax if applicable).

Prices subject to change based on reprints and revisions.

Thank you for your order!